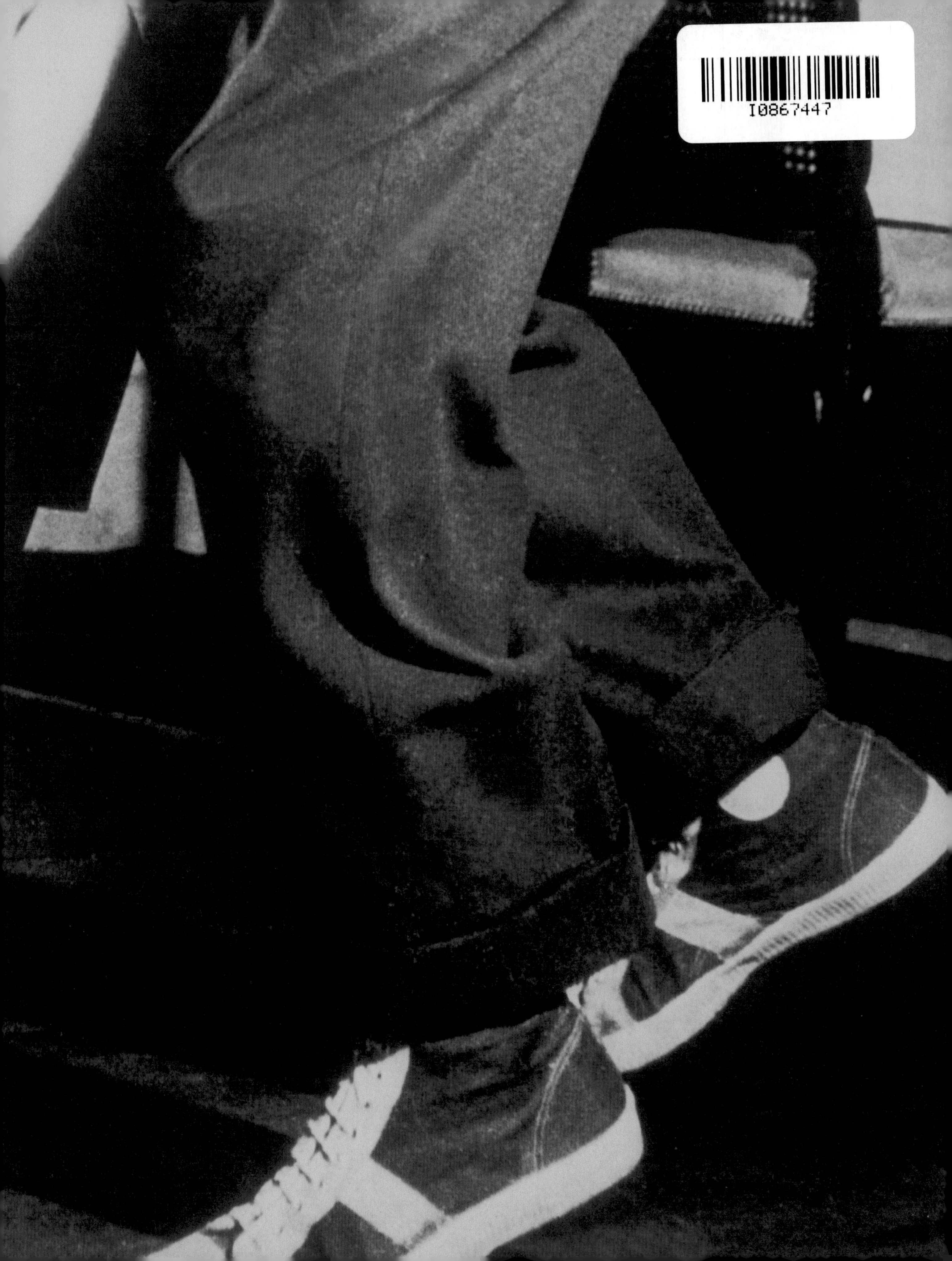

I0867447

ELVIS PRESLEY
CHUCK BERRY IS ON TOP
Jerry Lee Lewis
Don't Be Cruel
Goodnight Irene
Put Me Down
It All Depends
Ubangi Stomp
Crazy Arms
Jambalaya
Fools Like Me
High School Confidential
When The Saints Go Marching In
Matchbox
It'll Be Me
plus 6 bonus tracks!
"they're off and rolling," says Archie
THE EVERLY BROTHERS
The minute Bye-Bye Love hit, the Everlys were in. Frails sent mail by the bale. The same thing happened with Wake Up Little Susie – only more so. Their pickin' and singin' won everybody with an ear to hear. The whole country woke up and spoke up for the Everlys. That's why Archie brings you more of the kind of music that made them famous on this Cadence LP.
a high-fidelity recording by
CADENCE CLP-3003
CHUCK BERRY
one dozen berrys
THIS IS FATS
ROCK around the clock
BILL HALEY AND HIS COMETS
the fabulous
LITTLE RICHARD
AN ORIGINAL SOUNDTRACK RECORDING
ELVIS PRESLE
HAL WALLIS
KING CREOL
ELVIS
RCA VICTOR
LPM-1382
The "CHIRPING" CRICKETS
Rock'n Roll'n Robbins
Marty Robbins sings

That'll be the Day

THE BIRTH OF ROCK N' ROLL

Carolyn McHugh

sona BOOKS

sona BOOKS

© Danann Media Publishing Limited 2024

First Published Danann Media Publishing Limited 2024
WARNING: For private domestic use only, any unauthorised Copying, hiring, lending or public performance of this book is illegal.

CAT NO: SON0565

Photography courtesy of

Getty images:

Manchester Mirror/Mirrorpix
Daily Herald Archive
Hulton-Deutsch Collection/CORBIS
Watford/Mirrorpix/Mirrorpix
Bettmann
Joseph McKeown/Picture Post
PoPsie Randolph/Michael Ochs Archives
Harry Hammond/V&A Images
Gilles Petard/Redferns
GAB Archive/Redferns
Richi Howell/Redferns
George Rose
Colin Escott/Michael Ochs Archives
Jeffrey Mayer/WireImage
Michael Ochs Archives
James Kriegsmann/Michael Ochs Archives
CBS Photo Archive
Hulton Archive
Topical Press Agency
General Artists Corporation
Don Cravens
James Kriegsmann/Michael Ochs Archives
RB/Redferns
Nigel Osbourne/Redferns
Keystone-France/Gamma-Keystone
Movie Poster Image Art
Sunset Boulevard/Corbis
Dutch Scenery

Alamy:

Album
Everett Collection Inc
Trinity Mirror / Mirrorpix
Pictorial Press Ltd
Patti McConville
Mira
Barbara Ash

Other images, Wiki Commons

Book design Darren Grice at Ctrl-d
Proof reader Juliette O'Neil

All rights reserved. No Part of this title may be reproduced or transmitted in any material form (including photocopying or storing it in any medium by electronic means and whether or not transiently or incidentally to some other use of this publication) without the written permission of the copyright owner, except in accordance with the provisions of the Copyright, Designs and Patents Act 1988.Applications for the copyright owner's written permission should be addressed to the publisher.

Made in EU.
ISBN: 978-1-915343-22-2

Contents

Introduction

When rock and roll first exploded into the mainstream music scene in the mid-1950s, its effect was seismic. Nevertheless, it would have been hard to fathom the incredible contribution it would make to modern culture.

Having begun as simply a new style of music, rock and roll went on to influence fashion, film, art, and even language, as it took over the lives of impressionable young people around the world. Post-WW2, young people found themselves free from old expectations and with the time and money to indulge themselves. Rock and roll music was exciting and its lyrics, referencing youthful rebellion, young love, school and fast cars, really chimed with fans.

Boosted by the many technological advances of the era - including the electric guitar, the new 45rpm vinyl format, and inexpensive portable transistor radios - rock and roll music was available cheaply and easily.

The new sound, and its ground-breaking stars, made an incalculable contribution to music, which has inspired generations ever since, ensuring - as the 1958 Danny and The Juniors song puts it - 'Rock and roll is here to stay, it will never die... '

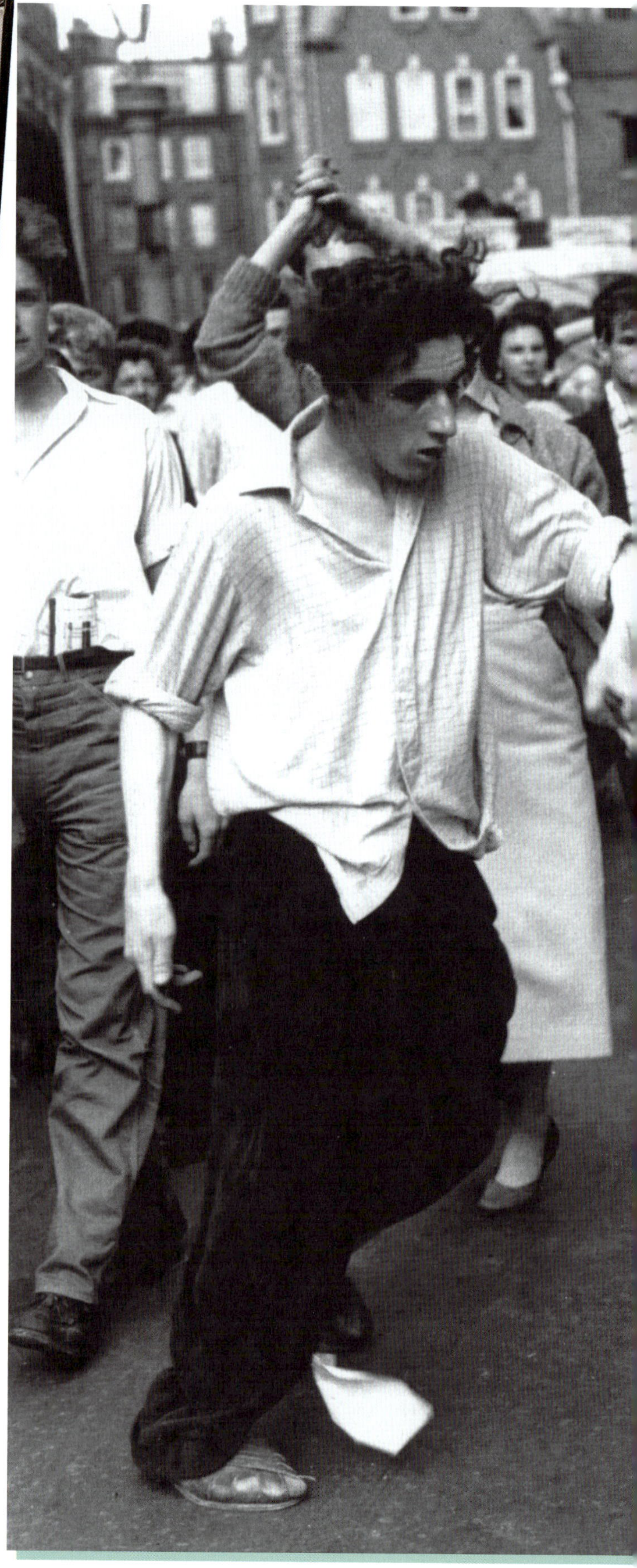

CHAPTER ONE

In The Beginning

1950s rock and roll was different and daring – music for the young, by the young. Teenagers loved it, their parents mostly didn't, while the status quo simply hated it. It felt new – and it was, although it hadn't happened overnight and was in fact born out of music from long before.

Rhythms and lyrics from gospel, blues, country, rockabilly, bluegrass, and jazz genres are all in the DNA of 1950s rock and roll.

But even before all of that, there was an African/American music form which undoubtedly influenced all the styles which led up to rock and roll. The fact that most Western popular music has its roots in African/American traditions, is a story fraught with complications in its telling. Although it seems incredible, it is true that music first made in the Mississippi Delta by black slaves and sharecroppers went on to profoundly impact on American and British white middle class teenagers of the 1950s. Such sad beginnings to an absolutely joyous period of music.

Handed down the generations, African/American music and culture went on to have profound influence worldwide, giving birth first to blues music, then in turn ragtime, jazz, swing, rhythm & blues (R&B) and soul.

However, the story of rock and roll proper actually starts in the 20th century, arising from the huge popularity of jazz and blues. One successful spin off from these styles was swing music, which being easier to move to, launched many dance crazes during the 1930s and 40s. In turn this led to early rhythm and blues (R&B), which was extremely

ABOVE: Portrait of Louis Jordan and his swing band, New York, between 1946 and 1948

LEFT: Okeh Records poster

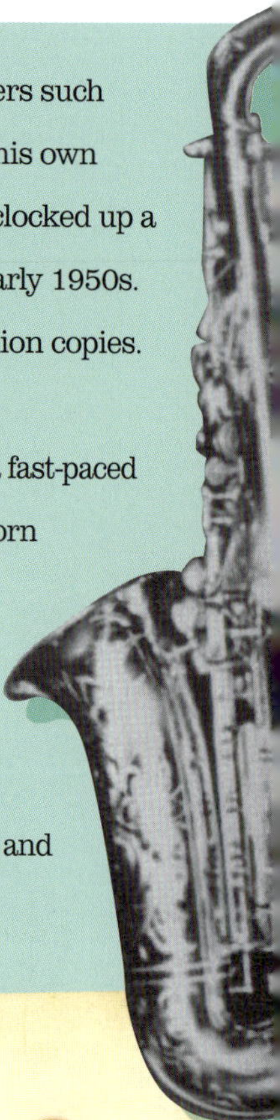

Louis Jordan

African/American saxophonist and singer

1908 - 1975

A huge influence on me when I started out…the real king of rock 'n' roll'

Elvis Presley

Louis Jordan was one of the most popular recording stars of the early 1940s and his energetic musical style was a huge influence on the rock and roll era which would follow.

Dubbed 'King of the Juke Box', Louis Jordan made his name playing jazz in the 1940s with famous bandleaders such as Chick Webb and Earl Hines. He then fronted his own band, Louis Jordan and his Tympany Five, and clocked up a string of hit singles during the late 1940s and early 1950s. His 1945 recording, Caldonia, sold over one million copies.

His music is sometimes described as jump blues, a fast-paced style of blues which is characterised by a strong horn and rhythm section. Jordan was an extremely influential figure and one of only a few black artists to successfully cross over from the old 'race charts' to the Billboard listings. Both Chuck Berry and Bill Haley were huge Louis Jordan fans and influenced by his music.

Listen to:

- Ration Blues
- Caldonia
- Saturday Night Fish Fry
- I'm Gonna Leave You on the Outskirts of Town

popular in the American black community, to the extent that R&B songs were first characterised as 'race records'.

The 78-rpms of blues, jazz and gospel music, known as 'race records', were specifically recorded by, and marketed to, African Americans in the early half of the 20th century. During those years, a time of segregation, the music that paved the way to rock and roll, promoted by companies including Okeh Records and Vocalion Records, was neither targeted at, nor largely appreciated by, white American audiences.

By degree it was R&B, again made for dancing, which evolved into rock and roll in the 1950s. The style of rock and roll was to retain the rhythm, and the blues, but with all its elements ramped up several notches. The sound was louder, the rhythms were stronger, the beats were heavier.

Dynamic young performers like Little Richard helped shape the driving rhythms that would come to define the rock and roll big beat. The new sound was also characterised by more sexualised lyrics and performances. The final factor propelling the new rock and roll sound to its worldwide popularity was that it was more commercial and, promoted by white musicians including Bill Haley and Elvis Presley, embraced by the youth of America's white middle classes.

When it all came together it was like nothing else. However, the shift from R&B to rock and roll was subtle and happened over several years. So vague is the map of the change in direction that music historians cannot even agree on what is officially the 'first' rock and roll song.

However, straw polls suggest that the song with the

ABOVE: Ike Turner's Kings Of Rhythm, BR L-R Jackie Brenston, Raymond Hill, Eddie jones, Fred Sample, Billy Gayles. FR L-R Jesse Knight Jr., Ike Turner, Eugene Washington, 1956

BELOW: Cadillac Boogie vinyl label

LEFT: A young Little Richard

ABOVE LEFT: 1951's Rocket 88 vinyl label

greatest claim, from a contested field, is 1951's *Rocket 88* written by Ike Turner (yes, that one) and recorded by him, with his saxophonist Jackie Brenston on vocals, billed as 'Jackie Brenston and his Delta Cats'. The 'rocket' in question was a superfast car of its day and the song it inspired was a mix of boogie and R&B. Its credentials as 'first rock and roll record' include its powerful and insistent backbeat together with use of a raw and distorted electric guitar.

While Brenston later claimed that the song was not original, saying that they had, 'simply borrowed from another jump blues about an automobile, *Cadillac Boogie*

by Jimmy Liggins [from 1947]', Ike Turner always maintained that he wrote the music and, together with his band The Kings of Rhythm, also wrote the lyrics.

Two other strong contenders for 'first rock and roll record', both from 1955 and both making the UK charts, are Bill Haley and His Comets *'Rock Around the Clock'* and Chuck Berry's *Maybellene*. But *Rocket 88* probably edges it by coming four years earlier and because Little Richard cited it as his inspiration to play the piano. In fact his 1958 recording of *Good Golly Miss Molly* reused the *Rocket 88* piano riff. Fats Domino's recording *The Fat* Man is also often referenced in the 'first record' debate, but probably just misses out by being more of a 'boogie-woogie' number. It is however a very important song, hugely influential on rock and roll and the first ever to sell one million copies.

ABOVE: Fats Domino, circa 1955

LEFT: Bill Haley and His Comets, L-R: Rudy Pompilli, Billy Williamson, Al Rex, Johnny Grande, Ralph Jones, Franny Beecher; Bill Haley is on top

TOP LEFT: Chuck Berry's Maybellene Vinyl label

So with the first recording sorted, the other key question concerns how rock and roll got its name. Again theories abound. Taking it chronologically, the first use of the term in print is attributed to music journalist Maurie Orodenker in his 1942 review of Lucky Millinder's song *Rock Me*, when he described Sister Rosetta Tharpe's featured vocals as 'rock-and-roll spiritual singing'. To be accurate, this song was so early that it doesn't qualify as a true rock and roll record, although it is part of the canon which came to influence 1950s rock and roll.

So taking a contemporaneous cue from someone heavily involved with the birth of rock and roll, the honour of naming rock and roll goes to Cleveland disc jockey Alan Freed who used the term during his radio shows. Freed is a key character in launching rock and roll and was a huge fan and promoter of the genre. In 1952 he even staged what many say was the first rock and roll stage show, the Moondog Coronation Ball in Cleveland Arena. 20,000 fans turned up at the 10,000 seat Arena, sealing the deal that rock and roll was the next big thing.

RIGHT: Lucky Millinder's song Rock Me Vinyl label
ABOVE: Sister Rosetta Tharpe

OTHER IMPORTANT RECORDINGS OF EARLY 1950S

1952

Lawdy Miss Clawdy
Lloyd Price

One of the biggest selling records of 1952, this track crossed over from R&B to new audiences, inspired many other songs and was recorded by various artists including Elvis Presley

1953

Crazy Man, Crazy
Bill Haley & His Comets

This track became the first rock and roll single to make the Billboard national chart.

1954

Shake, Rattle and Roll
Big Joe Turner and his Blues Kings

Championed by Alan Freed, Joe Turner had his first of 14 Top Ten R&B hits with *Shake, Rattle and Roll*. It made #1 on the R&B chart and #2 on the new pop chart. It would go on to be covered by Bill Haley and Elvis Presley.

ABOVE: Lloyd Price

LEFT: Big Joe Turner

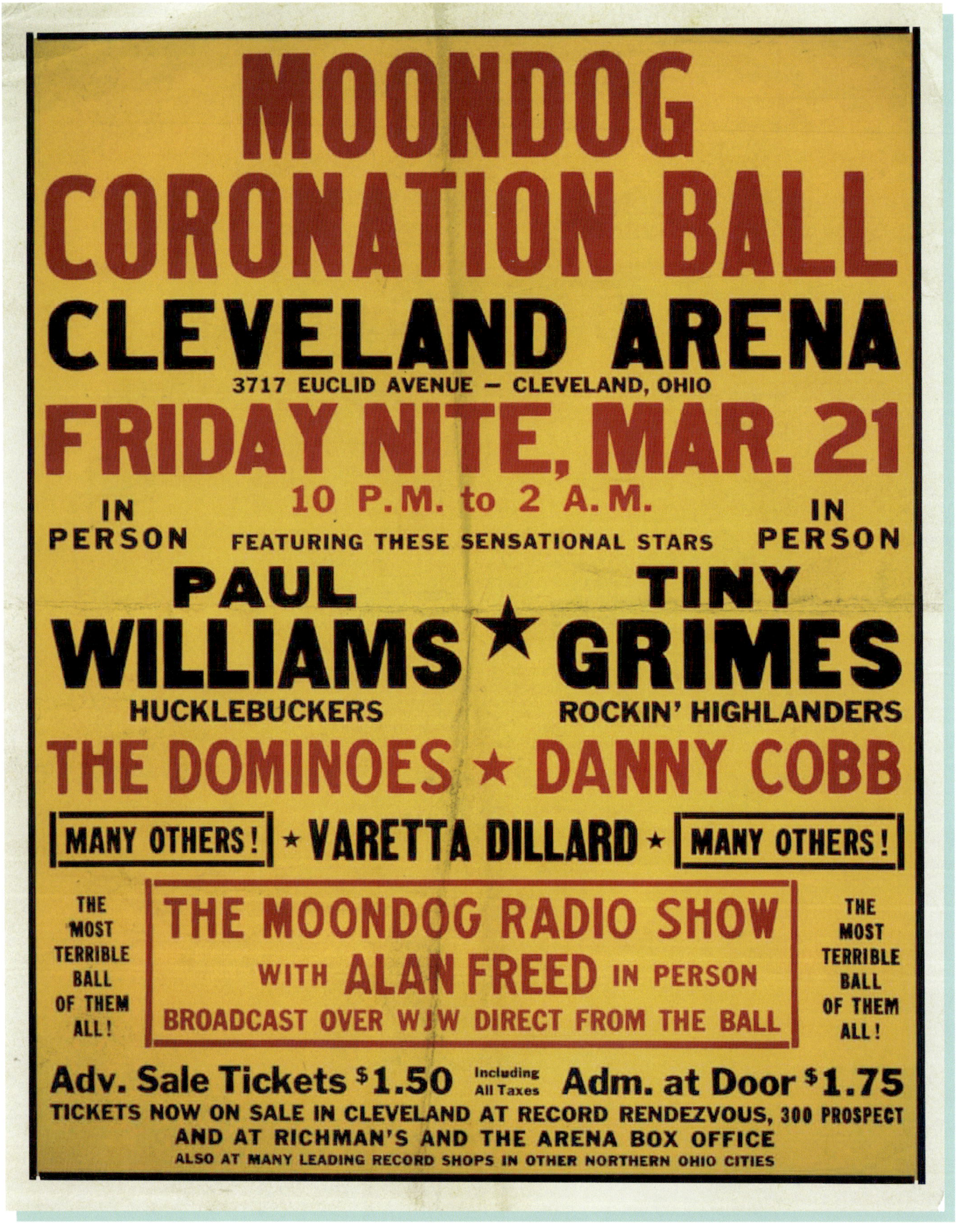
MOONDOG
CORONATION BALL
CLEVELAND ARENA
3717 EUCLID AVENUE – CLEVELAND, OHIO
FRIDAY NITE, MAR. 21
10 P.M. to 2 A.M.
IN PERSON
FEATURING THESE SENSATIONAL STARS
IN PERSON
PAUL WILLIAMS
HUCKLEBUCKERS
TINY GRIMES
ROCKIN' HIGHLANDERS
THE DOMINOES ★ DANNY COBB
MANY OTHERS! ★ VARETTA DILLARD ★ MANY OTHERS!
THE MOST TERRIBLE BALL OF THEM ALL!
THE MOONDOG RADIO SHOW
WITH ALAN FREED IN PERSON
BROADCAST OVER WJW DIRECT FROM THE BALL
THE MOST TERRIBLE BALL OF THEM ALL!
Adv. Sale Tickets $1.50 Including All Taxes Adm. at Door $1.75
TICKETS NOW ON SALE IN CLEVELAND AT RECORD RENDEZVOUS, 300 PROSPECT
AND AT RICHMAN'S AND THE ARENA BOX OFFICE
ALSO AT MANY LEADING RECORD SHOPS IN OTHER NORTHERN OHIO CITIES

ABOVE: Alan Freed with rock and roll musician Chuck Berry and publisher Gene Goodman during a radio interview and broadcast on September 6, 1955, New York

LEFT: Poster for the Moondog Coronation Ball

Freed said that the phrase 'rock and roll' was suggested to him because of the rolling and surging beat of the music.

Before then, the term 'rock 'n' roll' had traditionally been used to describe the up-and-down movement of an ocean-going ship. But over time it came to be used to describe a rollicking, song-filled ceremony, such as those in black churches, and then by others, quite differently, to describe the movements in sexual intercourse.

It was this link between rock and roll and sex that caused such a furore as the new music and its stars and roll exploded into the mainstream. Way before Elvis and his hips caused mayhem, early R&B stars had cleverly used slang terms to disguise frequent mentions of sex in their lyrics.

This daring rebellion was a big part of the appeal of early rock and roll as its fans enjoyed having something of their own which defied the old post-war mores.

As the hit 'Hairspray' song goes, *You Can't Stop the Beat* – and by the middle of the 1950s there was no denying rock and roll was casting its spell on American youth and about to dominate the music scene worldwide.

EARLY 20TH CENTURY TIMELINE

1920s

- Blues, known as 'the Devil's music', gains popularity
- Billboard, first founded as a trade magazine about billboard posters in 1894, evolved to become a music magazine and chart. In 1920 it appointed its first black music critic, James Albert Jackson, who wrote a column devoted to Afro/American performers

1940s

- Billboard begin tracking the best-selling records in its 'Chart Line' listing
- US involvement in WWII sees demise of big jazz bands in favour of smaller combos incorporating guitars, bass and drum
- Rise of independent labels and radio stations, delivering to more niche audiences begins
- Technology advances abound, leading to the development and spread of records (45rpm vinyl) amps, microphones and later the electric guitar

1930s

- Country, jazz, swing styles became popular
- Billboard introduce the first music 'hit parade' in 1936

Early 1950s

- Alan Freed, influential DJ and tireless promoter of the new rock and roll genre, begins playing black R&B for white listeners. He hosts the first rock and roll stage show, the Moondog Coronation Ball in Cleveland, Ohio in 1951
- Todd Storz, owner of radio station KOWH in Omaha, Nebraska, adopts a 'Top 40' format in 1953.

The Billboard
The World's Foremost Amusement

NOVEMBER 6, 1920 The Billboard

The NEGRO Actor, Actress Artist & Musician
Conducted By J.A. JACKSON
COMMUNICATIONS TO OUR OFFICES, 1493 BROADWAY, NEW YORK.

SALUTATION

INTEREST YOURSELF IN DEMAND

OUR INTEREST IN THE "MOVIES"

ABOVE: Alan Freed

ABOVE LEFT: Early RCA Victor 45rpm record player

LEFT: James Albert Jackson's first article for "The Billboard"

ABOVE: One of the very first concert posters to ever use the phrase "Rock and Roll" 1955

CHAPTER TWO

The Stage is Set

1954-55

1954 is widely considered the breakthrough year for rock 'n' roll in terms of tracks crossing over from the R&B charts to the new pop chart. Instrumental in this shift was, of course, Elvis Presley who recorded his cover of That's All Right Mama, originally a moderately successful, slower song, written and recorded by blues singer Arthur 'Big Boy' Crudup back in 1946. Some of the verses date back even further, as Crudup took lyrics first written by blues and gospel musician Blind Lemon Jefferson in 1926. For this reason, plus the fact it contains one of the earliest examples of a guitar solo break, the track is another sometimes mentioned as a contender for 'the first' rock and roll song.

But while the Elvis single was a regional hit and helped his early rise to fame as a local star in Memphis, it didn't make the national charts. But it wouldn't be long before Elvis broke through and became globally famous.

To fully understand why it took Elvis, a white boy, to popularise what was essentially black music and take it mainstream, it's important to consider the circumstances in America at that time.

ABOVE: Elvis' That's All Right Vinyl label
LEFT: Blind Lemon Jefferson
RIGHT: Alan Freed

It was only nine years since the end of the Second World War, during which the adult population of America and the UK had suffered and been unable to enjoy themselves in the way that the new breed of 1950s 'teenager' would.

Add to the mix that the civil rights movement was only in its infancy and many public schools remained segregated at that time. Rosa Parks was a year away from remaining in her seat on the bus and triggering the Montgomery bus boycott. And it would be almost another 10 years before Martin Luther King would give his 1963 'I Have a Dream' speech.

So the sad fact was that it took white musicians to make the new R&B-inspired rock and roll acceptable to the masses. And even then it wouldn't be easy. Society was on the verge of change, but progress was slow.

It was to rock and roll's advantage that its fans were teenagers. Post the horrors and deprivations of the Second World War, young people had new opportunities, brighter prospects and extra leisure time. Although they were still required to undertake national service, teenagers were otherwise emerging as a distinct socio-economic group. Rock and roll allowed them to celebrate living in post-war prosperity, free to enjoy a more liberal and carefree time than their parents.

However, given the times of societal change, it's not surprising that the new rock and roll sound and culture had many detractors, including outraged and nervous parents, religious organisations, and industry experts.

Radio was the medium which really introduced rock and roll, as its programme presenters, recently christened DJs, championed the new music of the early 1950s.

Although most of them couldn't play an instrument themselves, they recognised when a track or an artist had that indefinable 'something' and were respected purveyors of musical taste.

Chief among the crew of DJs filling the airwaves in the 1950s was Alan Freed (1922-1965). He gave rock and roll its name and a route to the masses via his late night radio show, and later took it to the stage and screen. From popularizing the R&B records that became the foundation of rock, to planning the first rock and roll concert, Alan Freed was a particular fan of Chuck Berry

and Fats Domino and can take credit for boosting their careers in the early days. As rock & roll took its first steps towards chart domination, earlier mainstream music became less appealing. The soft, crooning ballads by singers like Frank Sinatra, Bing Crosby and Perry Como lost popularity next to the revolutionary sounds of the new rock and roll artists.

OTHER JOCKS

Other DJs flying the flag for early rock and roll included:

Douglas 'Jocko' Henderson

Known as the 'Ace from Outer Space' thanks to his 1954 'Rocket Ship Show' broadcast every weeknight from New York. He helped popularise the now common style of DJ-chat, talking into the records, rolling his Rs and using rhyming patter.

Dewey Phillips

Famous for his Red, Hot and Blue radio show, was the first DJ to play Elvis, thanks to his friendship with Sam Phillips of Sun Records (no relation).

Although it wouldn't be a #1 hit until its re-release the following year, the pioneering track *Rock Around the Clock* was first recorded in April 1954 by Bill Haley and His Comets.

Written by Max C. Freedman and James E. Myers (under the pseudonym Jimmy De Knight) this 12-bar blues format tune was first recorded by an Italian/American novelty band called Sonny Dae and his Knights but only had modest success in the band's local area of Richmond, Virginia. Bill Haley and His Comets recorded their version in 1954 for Decca following a successful venture into the charts with *Crazy Man, Crazy* in 1953.

The song was originally titled *We're Gonna Rock Around the Clock Tonight!* later shortened to *(We're Gonna) Rock Around the Clock* and finally just *Rock Around the Clock.*

FAR LEFT: Douglas 'Jocko' Henderson
LEFT: Dewey Phillips
ABOVE: Sonny Dae and his Knights

BELOW: Bill Haley and His Comets

Its eventual success would make Bill Haley rock and roll's first major white star – although he would be eclipsed by Elvis Presley pretty quickly, he does at least hold the honour of pre-dating him.

The other key musical figures of that time were Fats Domino and Chuck Berry who, in their different ways, were both key in laying the groundwork and foundations on which rock and roll was built.

They had different instruments and styles. While pianist Fats was humble and unostentatious, guitarist Chuck was sassier and showier. But what they did have in common was incredible talent and a collection of early hit songs, making them the first black artists to gain popularity among white audiences. Many of their records went on to become classics.

The explosive and distorted guitar sound Chuck Berry used for his first hit *Maybellene* has influenced musicians ever since. Released in 1955, Maybellene is considered pioneering, with Rolling Stone magazine asserting that 'rock and roll guitar starts here'.

Making his mark with a different instrument, pianist Fats Domino was similarly innovative and made an incredible contribution to rock and roll piano. His biggest hit, the 1956 benchmark cover of *Blueberry Hill,* is now a rock and roll standard. It had originally been published and recorded in 1940, but Fats' new and definitive version slayed all that had come before and was one of the biggest hits of 1956, reaching #2 in the American charts.

LEFT: Elvis Presley with his back up singers "The Jordanaires" on stage in 1956

Listen to:

Ain't That a Shame

Blueberry Hill

I'm Walking

Fats Domino

American singer and pianist born Antoine Domino Jr.

1928 - 2017

'A huge influence on me when I started out…the real king of rock 'n' roll'

Elvis Presley

Before Little Richard and Jerry Lee Lewis, there was Fats Domino. This outsized singer and piano player was a rock and roll pioneer, whose innovative sound formed the very foundations of 1950s rock and roll. Yet despite Fats incredible contribution to rock and roll piano, his role as an early rock and roller is often under-appreciated. Even Fats himself didn't consider his music to be rock and roll, saying that 'it wasn't anything but the same rhythm and blues I'd been playing down in New Orleans'.

While that's as maybe, Fats did influence so many of the rock and roll stars which followed in his wake .. from Elvis to the Beatles.

Born in New Orleans to parents of Creole origin, Fats showed his musical talents at an early age and was performing by the time he was 10 years old. His father was a violinist and his brother in law Harrison Verrett, who was a jazz banjo player, taught him to play piano in the late 1930s.

Within a few years Fats was confident enough to start playing in local bars in New Orleans. It was around this time that he got the name Fats, suggested by a local bandleader he played with called Billy Diamond. It is said to have come to him partly because of his large appetite, but also in recognition of his talents being similar to those of Fats Waller, a successful jazz pianist from an earlier era.

With his unique style of R&B, which incorporated jive, jazz, jump blues and boogie woogie piano, Fats Domino quickly became a popular performer and had already become an R&B star in his hometown when he released his first single in December 1949. This debut single, *The Fat Man*, is credited by some as the first ever rock and roll record – it was certainly the first to sell one million copies – reaching #2 on the R&B chart.

Buoyed by this success as rock and roll took off, Fats became a major star round the world. Accomplished on the piano and with a powerful mellow voice and Creole drawl, he had a string of hit records. His biggest hit was the up-tempo *Blueberry Hill*, released in 1956, which reached #2 in the Top 40 chart for three weeks and #1 in the R&B chart for 11 weeks.

Fats often partnered with band leader and trumpet player Dave Bartholomew, who had co-written and produced *The Fat Man*. In a career which lasted 50 years, Fats sold a total of 65 million records and won 25 'gold records' – an award given when 500,000 units of a single or album are shipped to retailers.

In recognition of his influence and contribution to rock and roll, Fats received a Grammy Lifetime Achievement Award and was inducted into the Rock and Roll Hall of Fame in 1986. In 1998 he was presented with the National Medal of Arts from then President Bill Clinton.

ABOVE & RIGHT: Fats Domino concert posters

HOLCOMBS BALLROOM
Fork Plain Rd. Vancouver
Dancing 9 to 1 a.m.
MON. AUG. 31st
In Person!
Fats
"Goin' Home"
Domino
and his
GREAT ORCHESTRA
"Blueberry Hill"
"Margie"
I'm Ready"
"I Want to Walk You Home"
"My Blue Heaven"
Promotion: SCHWARTZ ENTERPRISES, 327 22nd Street, Oakland 12, California — Phone GLencourt 2-3361
TILGHMAN PRESS - 1201 - 32ND ST., OAK.

Chuck Berry

American musician born

Charles Edward Anderson Berry

1926 - 2017

'If you tried to give rock and roll another name, you might call it Chuck Berry'

John Lennon

Highly praised as 'the father of rock and roll', Chuck Berry's influence on rock and roll was hugely important – not least for his way with words.

Life magazine described him as 'rock's first poet, spinning three-minute sagas of teen angst'. As one of the first rock and roll songwriters to come up with most of his own material, Chuck was skilled at tapping into the lives of American teenagers and singing about what was important to them. Driving the lyrics were some of rock's immortal melodies, with guitar licks (and piano riffs from Johnnie Johnson).

Merging hillbilly country, urban blues and hot jazz styles onto his electric guitar, in a seemingly effortless 'pickin' style, Chuck was a pioneer of rock and roll instrumentation and rhythm. His guitar sound came to define rock and roll.

He is also key among the band of early rock and rollers responsible for giving rock and roll its 'ego'.

An accomplished showman, he was mesmerising on stage with his leering grins, mock-defiant stares and his famous 'duck walk' . Some commentators say he promoted the very 'idea' of rock and roll. Certainly he is known to have been a major influence on some of the biggest musicians to follow him, including John Lennon, Bruce Springsteen and Keith Richards.

Having grown up in a segregated middle class neighbourhood listening to blues, gospel and country music, Chuck had learned guitar in his teens, a period which also included a three year stint in jail for stealing cars.

Back in Civvy street, he managed to get some gigs in St Louis bar bands, eventually joining the house band at the Cosmopolitan Club, as a guitarist, before starting his own group, the Chuck Berry Combo. In 1955 Chuck signed with Chess Records and released *Maybellene* which kicked off his career proper, topping the R&B chart and reaching no 5 in the US.

His most recognisable hit is *Johnny B. Goode* from 1958. Although it wasn't his highest-charting hit, it has become the most iconic and enduring. The number enjoyed a further burst of popularity 30 years later when it was featured in the hit film 'Back to the Future', as performed by lead character Marty McFly who has time-travelled from 1985 to a high school prom in 1955, three years before the song was actually a hit. Marty introduces the number as '...an oldie – where I come from' and after his performance leaves the audience dumbstruck said, 'I guess you guys aren't ready for that yet – but your kids are going to love it'.

Other brushes with the law later in Chuck's career over possession of drugs and for taking an underage girl over the state line, sealed his 'bad boy' reputation.

Listen to:

Maybellene

Johnny B. Goode

Sweet Little Sixteen

No Particular Place to Go

Watch:

Hail! Hail! Rock 'n' Roll

A 1987 documentary made to celebrate Chuck's 60th birthday

ABOVE: Rock and roll musician Chuck Berry does the splits as he plays his Gibson hollow-body electric guitar, circa 1968

CHAPTER THREE

Controversy

AS ROCK AND ROLL TAKES HOLD

Along with many early rock and roll pioneers, Chuck Berry became known for songs which were playful and witty, risqué and ribald. This didn't play well with the mores of the time and attracted opprobrium from many different branches of the American establishment.

In September 1954, a *Billboard* magazine editorial called '*Control the Dimwits*' urged that jukeboxes be stripped of any R&B records with sexual double entendres. Their call was endorsed by The Songwriters Protective Association.

Variety magazine joined the fray the following year with several editorials concerned about the influence of rock and roll. One entitled 'A Warning to the Music Business', outlined a particular concern that the emerging genre of rock and roll would lead to the 'total breakdown of all

'PUT A NICKEL IN THE JUKEBOX AND LET THAT RECORD SPIN'

Once the centrepiece of pubs and cafés, now almost museum pieces, juke boxes are 'pay to play' machines full of vinyl 45 rpm records where the user chooses the song of their choice and pays for it to be played by inserting a coin. Each record was labelled with a letter and a number, A1, B20 and so on.

Long before the days of personalised playlists, the chosen song would play out to the whole venue. Customers would hear other people's choices as well as their own.

They were revolutionary when first launching in the late 1930s and hit their heyday in the 1950s. The 'juke' in their name is said to come from the word 'jook' which was a slang term for dancing and acting wildly.

reticence about sex' through lyrics mentioning 'hugs' and 'squeezes' as euphemisms for lovemaking. Urging self-restraint and responsibility from all involved in the music business, *Variety's* warning was picked up and published by various news outlets. That same year The Juvenile Delinquency and Crime Commission in Houston, Texas ran an anti-rock and roll crusade pressurising radio stations to ban records with 'lewd or suggestive' lyrics.

The American Society of Composers, Authors, and Publishers often slated rock and roll songs, perhaps because they had a vested interest. Most rock and roll performers were writing their own material so that professional songwriters were losing work. ASCAP member Billy Rose famously described rock and roll songs as 'in many cases, obscene junk, much on the level with dirty comic magazines.'

ABOVE: Chuck Berry

Bo Diddley

American songwriter and guitarist

1928 - 2008

'I opened the door for a lot of people, who just ran through and left me holding the knob'
Bo Diddley himself

Another primordial figure in 1950s music was Bo Diddley, a contemporary of Chuck Berry. Although he made more impression on the dedicated R&B charts than on rock and roll and pop music sales, his talents influenced countless other musicians who went on to be better remembered than he.

Despite his originality and exciting contribution to early rock and roll, for which he would eventually be honoured, Bo Diddley would frequently rail against the music business, and industry in which he had felt underappreciated and underpaid. At the heart of his frustration was the fact that he earned no royalties from the songs that he felt white artists had appropriated as they crossed over more successfully from R&B to the main charts.

He was inducted into the Rock and Roll Hall of Fame in 1987, added to the Hollywood Walk of Fame in 1989 and given lifetime achievement awards by the Rhythm & Blues Foundation in 1996 and the Grammys in 1998.

'But it didn't put no figures in my chequebook', he said. 'It just told people they thought enough of Bo Diddley for me to be honoured by putting my name on something, which was really great. But it didn't put no bucks in my kitty.'

Following a decade of playing on the streets and in the clubs and bars of Chicago, Bo Diddley got his big break early in 1955 when he released his double A-side single *Bo Diddley/I'm A Man* via Checker Records, a subsidiary of the influential Chess Records. While it was an immediate success, making #1 on the R&B chart, afterwards he only made the charts a handful more times, a fact that belies his massive and enduring influence. At the time he had a seminal effect on the artists coming up just behind him, including Elvis Presley and Buddy Holly, and even later on 1960s bands such as The Rolling Stones and The Yardbirds

Fans point to his innovative trademark rhythm, (known as hambone) the signature reverb effects he produced on his custom-built Gretsch guitar, and his wild on-stage performances - during which he would sometimes even rap - as proof positive that he should be included in any retrospective appreciation.

Listen to:

- Bo Diddley
- Who Do You Love
- Mona
- Crackin' Up
- Say Man
- Ride On Josephine
- Road Runner

Penalty of the Law

ABOVE: Bo Diddley with his band, including the Duchess aka Norma Jean-Wofford on guitar and Jerome Green with maracas, pose for a portrait on a scooter in September 1959 in New York

Even celebrated crooner Frank Sinatra added to the opprobrium facing rock and roll, saying that the kind of music Elvis sang was 'deplorable ...a rancid smelling aphrodisiac...it fosters almost universally negative and destructive directions in young people'.

Among the many other controversies and censorship efforts during the early rock and roll years were cancellations of concerts due to possible violence, most famously a Fats Domino concert in Bridgeport, Connecticut in May 1955.

Then the film 'Blackboard Jungle' – featuring a rock and roll theme tune - was banned. This 1955 melodrama starring Glenn Ford told the story of a new English teacher joining an inner-city school where anti-social behaviour runs rife. The plot charts his efforts to do a good job, despite resistance from his faculty and his class of unruly, ethnically diverse students.

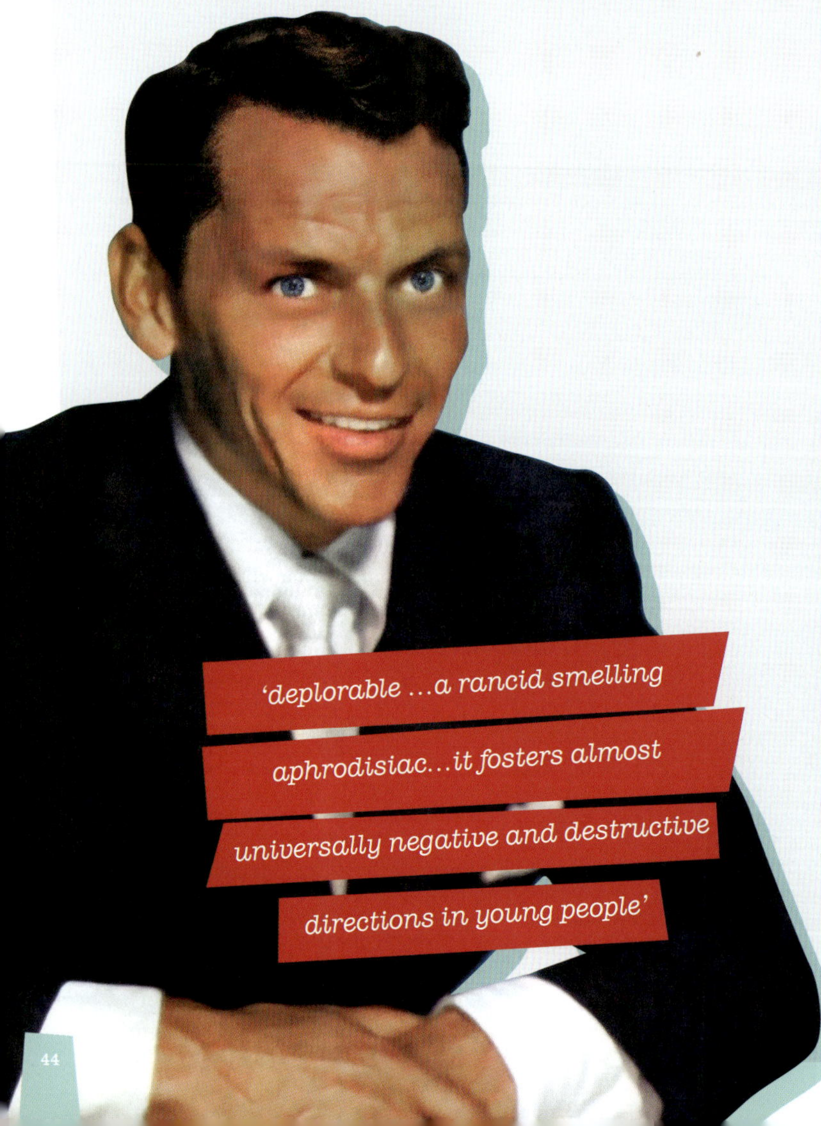

Tense and hard-hitting, the film's unflinching depictions of teenage angst, racial conflict and juvenile violence caused outrage at the time. Released during the very early days of rock and roll, when the sound was stirring up controversy, the film's director Richard Brooks made the bold move of choosing the innovative *Rock Around the Clock* by Bill Haley and His Comets as the film's opening and closing soundtrack. It had absolutely no connection to the rest of the film, but crowds of people left the cinema singing it and the association was to be everlasting.

Serving as an anthem for rebellious youth, the track entered the rock and roll history books as being the first track of its type to be used in a hit Hollywood film. Boosted by the surrounding publicity, *Rock Around the Clock* stayed at #1 for two months and reached #3 on the R&B chart. Before this the track had been the B-side to *Thirteen Women (and Only One Man in Town)* and achieved respectable, if unremarkable, sales of 75,000 copies.

The now world-famous track, widely considered the song that propelled rock and roll into the mainstream, might have been forgotten had director Richard Brooks not overheard it one night when visiting the home of his star Glenn Ford when Glenn's son Peter was listening to it. Its use in the film represented the first time that rock and roll was officially linked in popular culture with the emerging 'generation gap' between parents who had suffered in the war and their children, who were generally living a more carefree and prosperous life. The overall effect was to cement in the minds of the older generation the perceived link between rock and roll music and juvenile delinquency.

As one of the first major rock 'n' roll hits, making number one in both the American and British charts in 1954, *Rock Around the Clock* is a good example of many other rock and roll songs of the time. A saxophone joins the guitars and drums as a prominent instrument and riffs run throughout the song. Many rock 'n' roll songs followed the same standard 12 bar blues chord structure. With its jump-band R&B beat, known as 'jump blues', a thumping double bass and twanging guitar breaks, the track marked a radical shift in American music and is justifiably ranked at 159 on Rolling Stone magazine's top 500 Greatest Songs of all Time. It also became the first million-selling single of its genre in the UK.

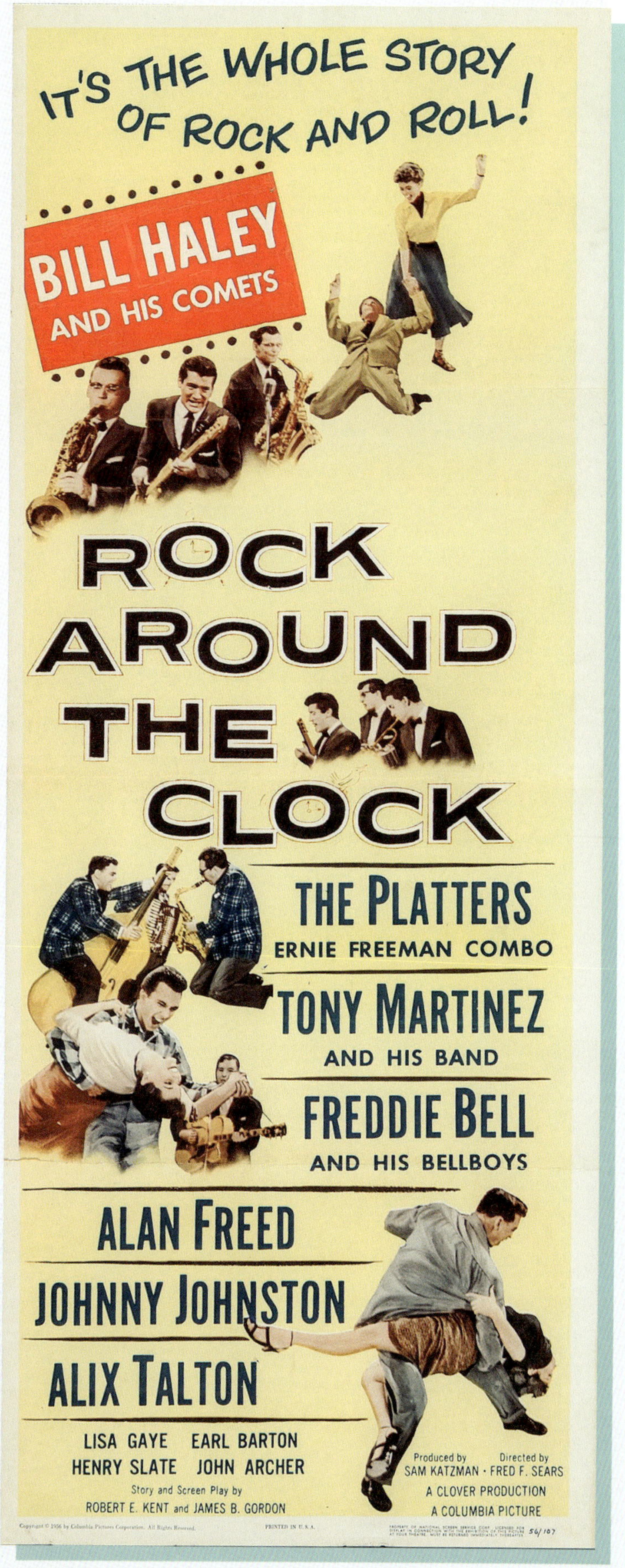

Bill Haley

American musician born William John Clifton Haley

1925 - 1981

'It didn't matter about the fame. He went out there and played'

Chuck Berry

The unlikely break out star of 1955 was the clean cut and avuncular 29-year-old Bill Haley who, just briefly, was the first rock and roll star before the top prize of rock and roll 'king' was taken by Elvis Presley.

Just pre-dating Elvis, Bill Haley and His Comets, who had already covered Ike Turner's *Rocket 88,* released the anthem *Rock Around the Clock* which assured them of a place in any history of rock and roll.

Already balding, Bill looked older than his 29 years. With a curl atop his face, he was certainly not moody like James Dean or a sex symbol like Marlon Brando - both big movie stars of the time. But when his track was used during the opening credits of the 1955 film 'Blackboard Jungle', it took off into the stratosphere of the charts and made #1 that July.

Originally set up as a bluesy country and western outfit called Bill Haley and the Saddlemen, the band's rock and roll career began with a cover of Ike Turner's *Rocket 88* which was recorded on the Holiday Records label in 1951. This sold well and was followed up in 1952 with a cover of a 1940s R&B song *Rock the Joint*. There was a feeling that the band needed a new name to reflect its new sound and the story goes that a friend of Bill's suggested adopting 'The Comets' as a nod to Halley's Comet, which although pronounced differently (to rhyme with 'valley' rather than Bill's surname Haley which rhymed with 'Bailey') also incorporated the fiery nature of their music. The band duly changed its name in 1952.

Soon after renaming the band - the original Comets line-up included pianist and accordion player Johnny Grande, guitarist Billy Williamson and bass player Marshall Lytle - Bill added to its number by hiring its first fulltime drummer, Dick Richards. One other change to their sound came about when pianist Johnny Grande switched to playing the accordion during live shows as it was more portable and also allowed him to move around more during the dance numbers.

Newly named, the band clocked up its first national hit record in 1953 with an original number, written by Bill, called *Crazy Man, Crazy*, reportedly inspired by an overheard audience comment. This led to their being signed up by Decca Records, for whom they recorded Rock Around the Clock in 1954, now with a tenor sax player Joey Ambrose joining the Comets. The number was only a modest success at first and while it ticked along it was overtaken by the band's cover of Big Joe Turner's *Shake, Rattle and Roll* – a million seller.

But eventually, after making its name following its use as the soundtrack to the controversial film 'Blackboard Jungle', *Rock Around the Clock* would reign supreme as one of rock and roll's most significant recordings and biggest ever hits, with sales estimated at 25 million copies.

Topping the American musical charts that summer, the record kept the #1 spot for eight weeks and was the first rock and roll record to do so.

There were various changes to the band's line up over the years, and a later line up – Rudy Pompilli on sax, Al Rex on double bass, Charles Porter and Ralph Jones on drums and Franny Beecher on lead guitar - was the most popular and the one that appeared in the Bill Haley movies 'Rock Around the Clock' and 'Don't Knock the Rock'. In 1956, a knock-off movie entitled *Rock Around the Clock* featuring Haley, The Platters, Freddie Bell & the Bellboys and others was released, and the idea of jiving to the music in the cinema caught on around the country.

Among their other big hits were *See You Later, Alligator, Don't Knock the Rock, Rudy's Rock* and *Skinny Minnie*. But nothing ever came close to the success of *Rock Around the Clock* and being the first doesn't make you the biggest or most enduring talent. While his place in the history books was assured, Bill Haley's popularity began to wane as rock and roll moved to a wilder phase and bigger characters stars such as Elvis, Little Richard and Jerry Lee Lewis rose to incredible heights in the later 1950s. He kept recording and touring however, and remained a big selling concert performer in Europe throughout the 1960s as well as scoring Spanish language hits, thanks to Bill's proficiency as a Spanish speaker. As Bill Haley y sus Cometas, the band had hits including Twist Espanol and became famous for promoting the American dance craze, the Twist, in Mexico and Latin America.

ABOVE: Bill Haley And His Comets, perform on stage (L-R) Johnny Grande, Al Rex, Bill Haley, Ralph Jones, Rudy Pompilli (lying on stage playing saxophone), Franny Beecher, Billy Williamson, 6 February 1957

ABOVE & RIGHT: Bill Haley and the Comets concert posters

FIRST BIG NAME OF THE SEASON
OLD ORCHARD
PALACE
BALLROOM
TUESDAY, MAY 28
APPEARING IN PERSON
on DECCA RECORDS ★ GET THEIR NEW HITS!
BILL HALEY
and His COMETS
THE SHAKE RATTLE and ROLL BOYS
"RIP IT UP" ★ "SEE YOU LATER ALLIGATER" ★ "TEEN - AGER'S MOTHER"
"DIM DIM THE LIGHTS"
"ROCK AROUND THE CLOCK"
"ROCKIN' through the RYE"
"SHAKE RATTLE and ROLL"
Booking Direction: JOLLY JOYCE AGENCY - N. Y. C. & PHILA.
DESIGN No 735 (14 x 22)
U. S. A.
POSTERS INC., 835 Cherry St., Phila.

CHAPTER FOUR

THINGS GET *Loud & Lairy*

With Fats Domino, Chuck Berry and Bill Haley having paved the way, the ground was set for the next stage of rock and roll. It would be wilder, raunchier than before and spearheaded by the fiery superstar Little Richard, a singer/songwriter /pianist extraordinaire.

When he first hit the scene in 1955, screaming and showy, he was a true original. He was fond of describing himself as rock and roll's true 'king', but while he was indeed incredibly influential, it should be noted that by the time he had his first big hit with *Tutti Frutti*, Fats Domino and Bill Haley were already stars and Elvis Presley and Chuck Berry had had their first hits.

Little Richard can however take credit for kick-starting rock and roll with a persona no one had seen before. A mixed race, bisexual performer, his feminine demeanour made him an androgynous figure, slightly built, with mascara on his lashes and pompadour hair piled upon his head. Both his lyrics and piano playing was bizarre – usually standing, he'd sometimes play with his back to the piano and arms behind him, other times he'd be playing with one leg above the keyboard resting on the case. Grinning and rolling his eyes, he'd belt out his songs with zeal, occasionally employing falsetto as he shook his head from side to side in a style the Beatles would later mimic.

The influence exerted by Little Richard is simply staggering. Credited as being the 'architect of rock and roll' and described by an admiring Elvis as 'the greatest', he created the new 'rules' of rock and roll – number one of which was, 'Be Loud!'

He had a trademark formula of three chords played with a contagious, driving rhythm and blues feel.

Without ever having seen him in person, modern music fans will have witnessed elements of his dramatic, energetic, and extravagant performances and unique vocal style as they popped up again in the performances of musicians he influenced, including Paul McCartney, Jimi Hendrix and Prince. But in 1955 such flare and femininity had never before been seen in a male artist.

Brought up in the Baptist church, Little Richard combined religious gospel music with boogie-woogie and rhythm and blues to create his own fiery and unique sound, incorporating suggestive lyrics with a unique singing style.

ABOVE: Little Richard poses for a portrait, circa 1956, Hollywood

His religious and conservative upbringing had a lifelong effect on him as he spent his life trying to square the two incompatible sides of his personality – the god-fearing Baptist and the sex, drugs and rock and roller were completely at odds with each other. The result, particularly of his struggle with his homosexuality, was that on several occasions he renounced rock and roll and attempted a new life within the church.

He began his recording career in 1951, cutting eight urban blues tracks with his mentor Billy Wright and his orchestra. Most of these were unsuccessful, until in 1955 he recorded a dozen tracks with producer Robert (Bumps) Blackwell. This batch included the classic *Tutti Frutti* and the rest is history as the song gave Richard his first R&B and hit in the USA and launched him into an unsuspecting world.

Although the song had been part of his stage act for some time, the sexual nature of its lyrics meant that it would never have been released or promoted as a single. However, during the recording session with Robert Blackwell, it was decided that the song was so good that, with sanitised lyrics, it could work as a release. Songwriter Dorothy LaBostrie cleaned up the song - for example substituting 'booty' for 'rooti' and it became a major hit. Richard's upbeat, energetic rendition of somewhat gibberish lyrics was instantly popular and his opening cry of 'Awop-Bop-a-Loo-Mop, Alop-Bam-Boom' became a clarion call to rock and rollers everywhere which has kept its appeal ever since.

LEFT: Little Richard performing, circa 1956
RIGHT: Dorothy LaBostrie
ABOVE RIGHT: Original release of Here's Little Richard

'booty' for 'rooti'

IN PERSON
"Lucille"
LITTLE
RICHARD
"LONG TALL SALLY"
"TUTTI FRUITTI"
and his ORCHESTRA
GLOBE POSTER - BALTIMORE

He followed it up with a string of hit singles between September 1955 and October 1957 including *Lucille, Long Tall Sally, Slippin' and Slidin'* and *Good Golly Miss Molly* and a top 20 album *Here's Little Richard,* before astounding the industry and devastating his fans by giving it all up to study theology. This was one of several attempts to overcome his demons and devote himself to the church. He was persuaded to return to the secular scene in 1962, touring England amongst other things. He was eventually ordained as a minister in 1970 and stepped into the church again fulltime in 1979 – a further illustration of his lifelong struggle to combine his love of rock and roll with the pull of his religious beliefs. The two did not make good bedfellows.

After spending time preaching, and even officiating at celebrity weddings and funerals, Richard was lured back to music after seeing the positive reaction and enticing offers of work following his 1986 induction into the Rock and Roll Hall of Fame and the publication of a successful biography 'The Life and Times of Little Richard'. But most memorably he re-emerged in the 1986 comedy 'Down and Out in Beverly Hills' playing Orvis Goodnight, a black

FAR LEFT: Original promo poster from the 1950s
ABOVE: Topps gum trading card of Little Richard In 1957
LEFT: Little Richard preaching in 1981 Oakland, California

record producer unhappy with the racism of the suburbs, and also singing *Great Gosh A'Mighty* on the soundtrack.

This was a fitting way to return as, some 30 years before, he had appeared in one of the earliest rock and roll movies, 'The Girl Can't Help It', also the title of his major hit. The power of rock and roll in movies had been obvious from the reaction to 'Blackboard Jungle'. Ever keen to ride the wave of a new trend, Hollywood set about creating this 1956 musical comedy featured blonde bombshell Jayne Mansfield as the 'girl' in question, Jerri Jordan, who in the film's iconic opening scene sashays along to the title track. She is the girlfriend of a retired gangster who hires a manager to make her a rock and roll star. 'The Girl Can't Help It' combined broad comedy with legendary rock and roll performances from Little Richard, who sings his hit song *Ready Teddy*, along with explosive cameos from other early rockers Eddie Cochran, Gene Vincent and Fats Domino among others. While not a vintage production in terms of its storyline, the film is still recognised and significant because it captured influential performances from these legendary artists in glorious DeLuxe Color and CinemaScope. The fact that the film captures influential performances from these legendary artists, including Eddie Cochran's hit *20 Flight Rock,* is the main reason for its recognition and significance. Music journalist and biographer Philip Norman credited the movie as the "most potent" celebration of rock music ever captured on film.

FAR LEFT: Little Richard poses for a portait, circa 1967

Little Richard

American musician, singer, and songwriter, born Richard Wayne Penniman

1932 - 2020

As James Brown once said;

'Little Richard put the funk in the rock and roll beat'

His 1955 hit Tutti Frutti includes the blaring volume and distinctive beat and rhythm which became definitive characteristics of rock and roll. The track is widely regarded as one of the recordings that 'changed the world' and delineated the advance from the old jump blues and hillbilly sound to the new 'rock and roll', with 'Awop-Bop-a-Loo-Mop, Alop-Bam-Boom' being noted by Rolling Stone magazine as 'the most inspired rock lyric ever recorded'. The line is believed to be the onomatopoeic verbalisation of a drum pattern that Richard had imagined.

Riding high in the charts from 1955 to 1957, Richard had a unique blend of powerful vocals, energetic delivery and mesmerising flamboyance as he pounced on his piano, pounding out songs that would become worldwide hits. He certainly impressed two young men on the other side of the Atlantic in Liverpool where a young Paul McCartney and John Lennon in their pre-Beatle days bonded over their mutual admiration for Richard and were inspired to follow his lead. Little did they suspect at the time that they would go on to play with him one day- in late 1962, as they were starting out, the Beatles opened for Little Richard at the Star-Club in Hamburg for 14 shows.

Richard did his best to combine his religious work with a recording career during his later years but major health setbacks, including a broken hip in 2009 and a heart attack in 2013, led to his eventual retirement. He died 9 May 2020 aged 87.

Watch:

The Girl Can't Help It

Don't Knock the Rock

Down and Out in Beverly Hills

Listen to:

- Tutti Frutti
- Long Tall Sally
- Ready Teddy
- Lucille
- Good Golly Miss Molly

ABOVE: Little Richard in Don't Knock The Rock, 1956

ABOVE: Elvis Presley and Sam Phillips eating ice cream and cake in 1956 in Memphis Tennessee

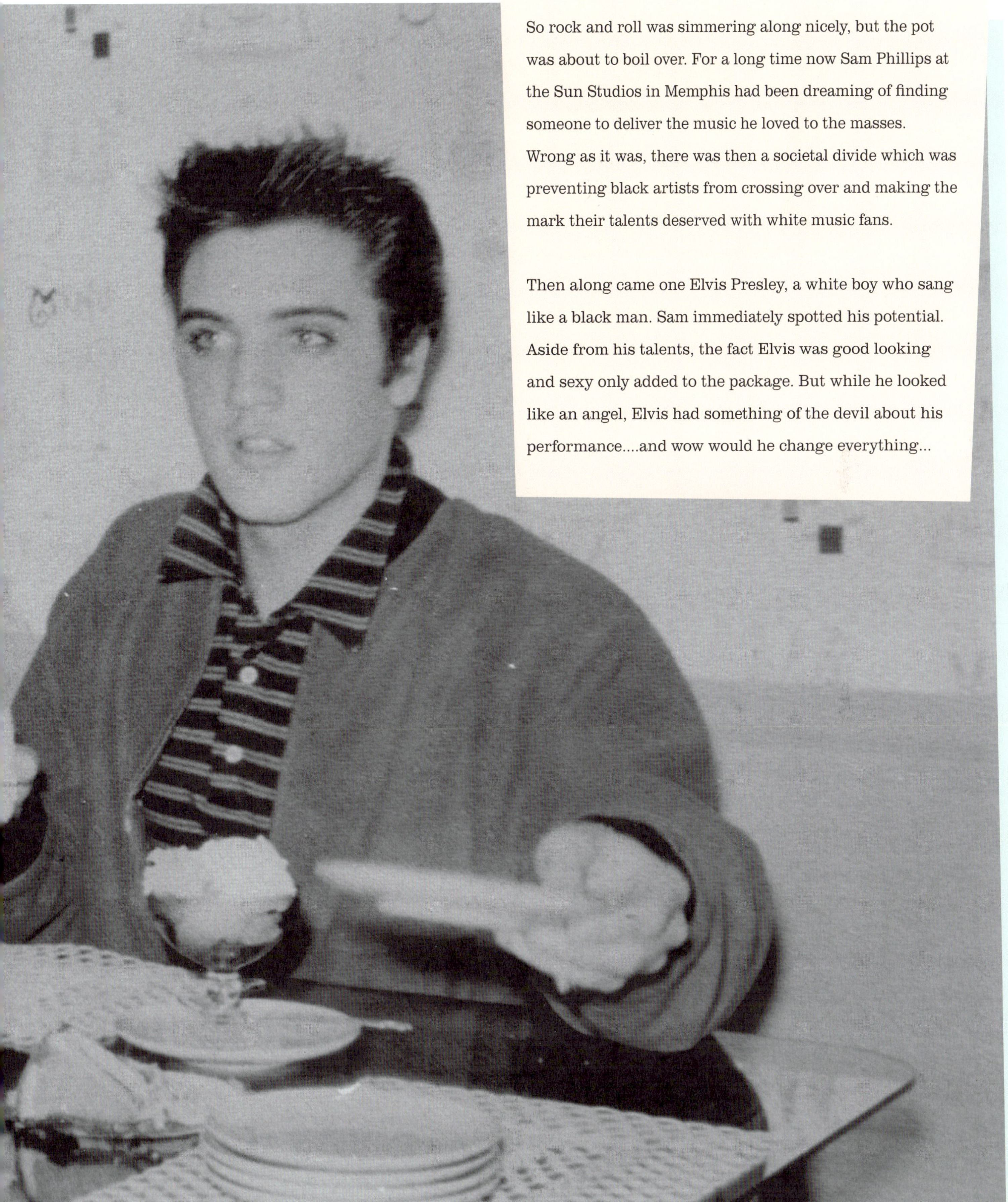

So rock and roll was simmering along nicely, but the pot was about to boil over. For a long time now Sam Phillips at the Sun Studios in Memphis had been dreaming of finding someone to deliver the music he loved to the masses. Wrong as it was, there was then a societal divide which was preventing black artists from crossing over and making the mark their talents deserved with white music fans.

Then along came one Elvis Presley, a white boy who sang like a black man. Sam immediately spotted his potential. Aside from his talents, the fact Elvis was good looking and sexy only added to the package. But while he looked like an angel, Elvis had something of the devil about his performance....and wow would he change everything...

CHAPTER FIVE

Elvis Presley

THE KING OF ROCK AND ROLL

'Elvis had everything, the looks, the moves, the manager and the talent.'

Carl Perkins, Elvis's contemporary, the writer and original singer of Blue Suede Shoes

Elvis Presley (1935-1977) was the world's first superstar and the biggest celebrity of the 20th century. As well as being a singer, actor, and cultural icon, he was among the most influential musicians ever. He was, and will forever be known as, 'The King of Rock and Roll', the musical genre which he popularised as he bridged the gap between early rock and pop music.

It is hard to overstate his impact on the popular culture of the 1950s and 60s, when his extraordinary talents and good looks – together with sexualised performances which scandalised middle America - made him a phenomenon as the pure embodiment of rock and roll. To this day he remains the most successful singles artist in UK chart history, with 18 number one hits, 76 Top 10s and 139 Top 40s.

Born into the poverty of East Tupelo, Mississippi, before finding his musical home in Memphis, Elvis grew up surrounded by gospel music, country and blues, genres which all influenced his own music and performances.

Although his background was poor, Elvis found there were tremendous riches in the music world and would listen avidly to the radio, absorbing all sorts of rhythms and styles from country, blues and gospel. Programmes featuring singers such as Sister Rosetta Tharpe and Arthur 'Big Boy' Crudup were popular choices and Elvis would also be sure to catch The Grand Ole Opry country show on a Saturday evening.

Elvis was 13 years old when his family moved to Memphis in 1948. The place was so different from Tupelo that it was almost the equivalent of moving to Paris. Memphis was much more affluent and cultured than his birthplace, full of life, and opportunities.

The city, with the powerful Mississippi river running through it, had attracted lots of new people from the southern states seeking better opportunities after World War Two. Key for Elvis, there was a big entertainment district, full of the sounds the city's new citizens had brought with them.

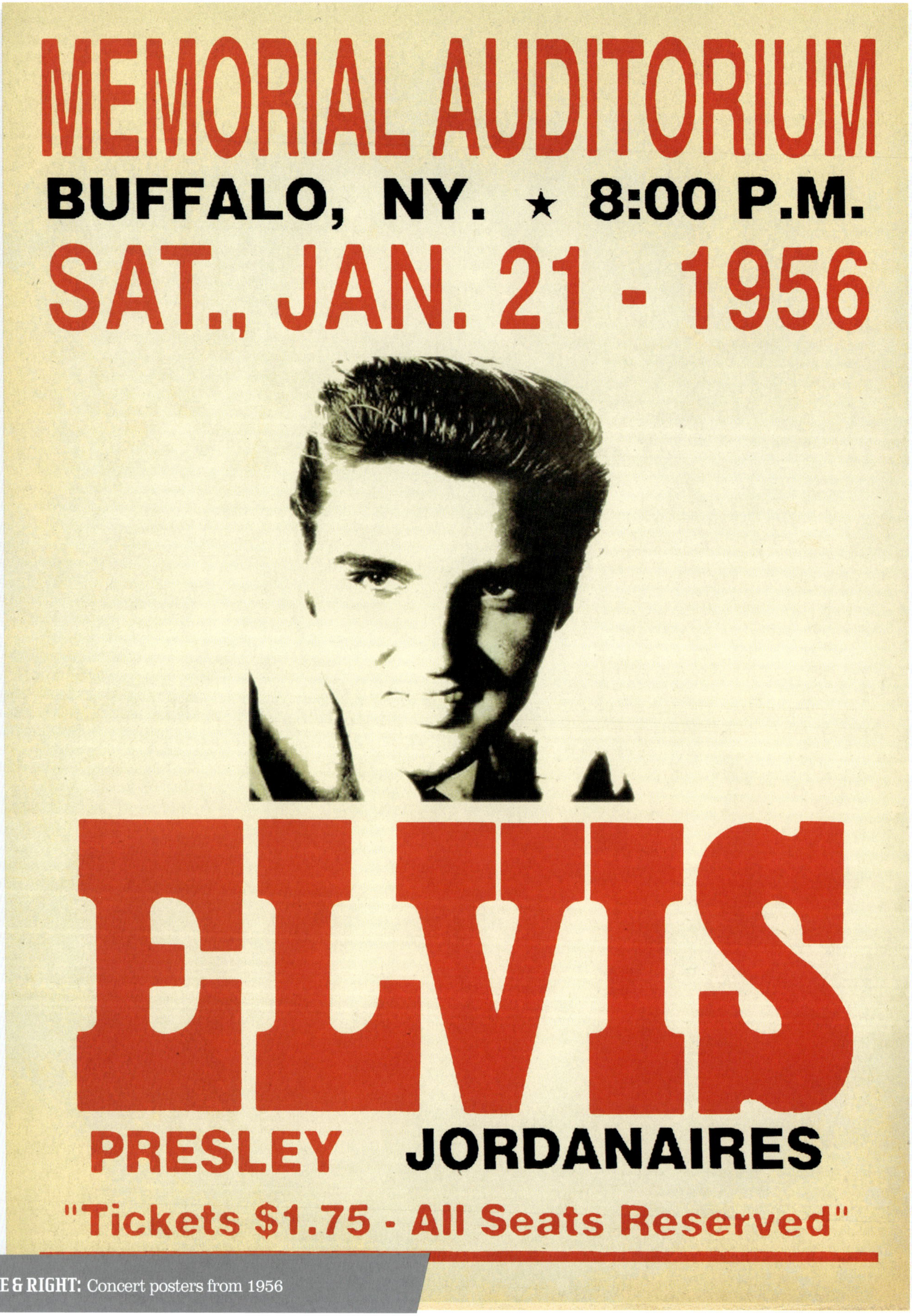

ABOVE & RIGHT: Concert posters from 1956

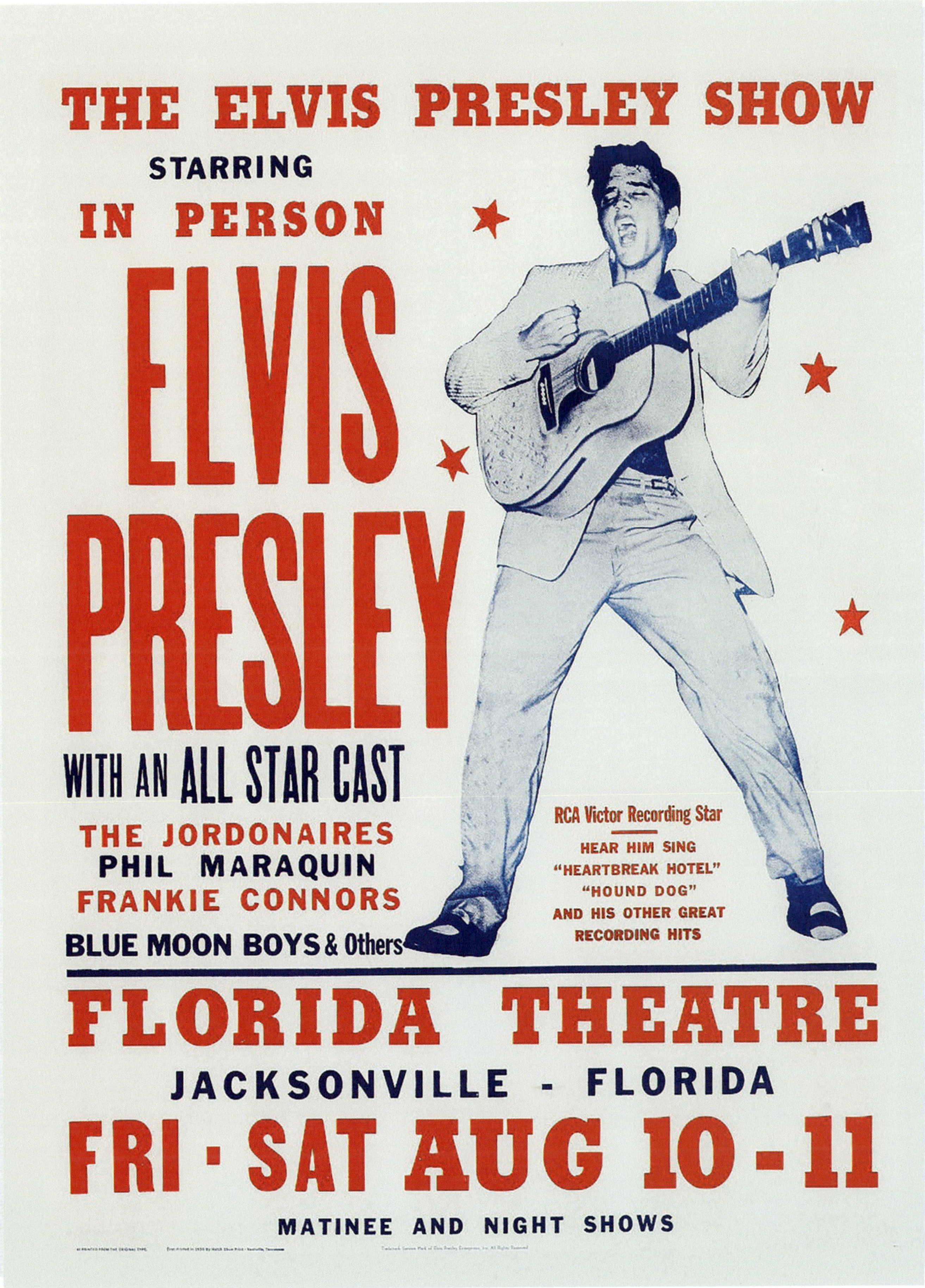
THE ELVIS PRESLEY SHOW
STARRING
IN PERSON
ELVIS
PRESLEY
WITH AN ALL STAR CAST
THE JORDONAIRES
PHIL MARAQUIN
FRANKIE CONNORS
BLUE MOON BOYS & Others
RCA Victor Recording Star
HEAR HIM SING
"HEARTBREAK HOTEL"
"HOUND DOG"
AND HIS OTHER GREAT
RECORDING HITS
FLORIDA THEATRE
JACKSONVILLE - FLORIDA
FRI · SAT AUG 10 - 11
MATINEE AND NIGHT SHOWS

Slowly he began to put together a version of himself which the world would come to know as 'Elvis'. He let his hair grow longer, formed it into a quiff and added sideburns as soon as he could. His childhood shyness seemed to have evaporated as he grew to find his place in life and now Elvis was happy to stand out from the crowd.

After school, his first job on an assembly line didn't last long, then he joined Crown Electric as an apprentice electrician for $3 an hour where his duties included driving a truck and helping the electricians pull wires.

It was while he was on the road that he began driving past the Memphis Recording Service, owned by Sam Phillips who was setting up a new label called Sun Records. Things were suddenly about to happen and, as it turned out, the closest young Elvis would get to qualifying as an electrician would be when he got on stage and began generating power of his own...

ABOVE: Elvis recording in an RCA Victor studio in 1956
MAIN IMAGE: Presley portrait in Memphis, Tennessee, 1956

Elvis found that, as his horizons expanded, his fortunes improved. His parents gave him what money they could for records and trips to music concerts. He loved going into central Memphis - the sounds, the sights and the bright lights excited him, and he became a willing student of music as he visited the clubs on Beale Street at the heart of the scene. He had eclectic taste and picked up influences from all around him, witnessing for example the talent of entertainers such as B.B. King and Rufus Thomas and noting their powerful connection with audiences.

Working with Sam Phillips, Elvis recorded numbers such as *That's All Right (Mama)* and *Blue Moon of Kentucky* before moving to the bigger label of RCA in 1955, where his success would become monumental. He would go on to score 18 number one hits including his first, *Heartbreak Hotel* in 1956, and his last, *Suspicious Minds* in 1969, with classics such as *Don't Be Cruel, Love Me Tender, It's Now or Never,* and *Are You Lonesome Tonight?* along the way.

Elvis was offered *Heartbreak Hotel* by its writers Tommy Durden and Mae Boren Axton. The song was gloomy and other singers had turned it down, including the Wilburn Brothers who thought it was 'strange and almost morbid'.

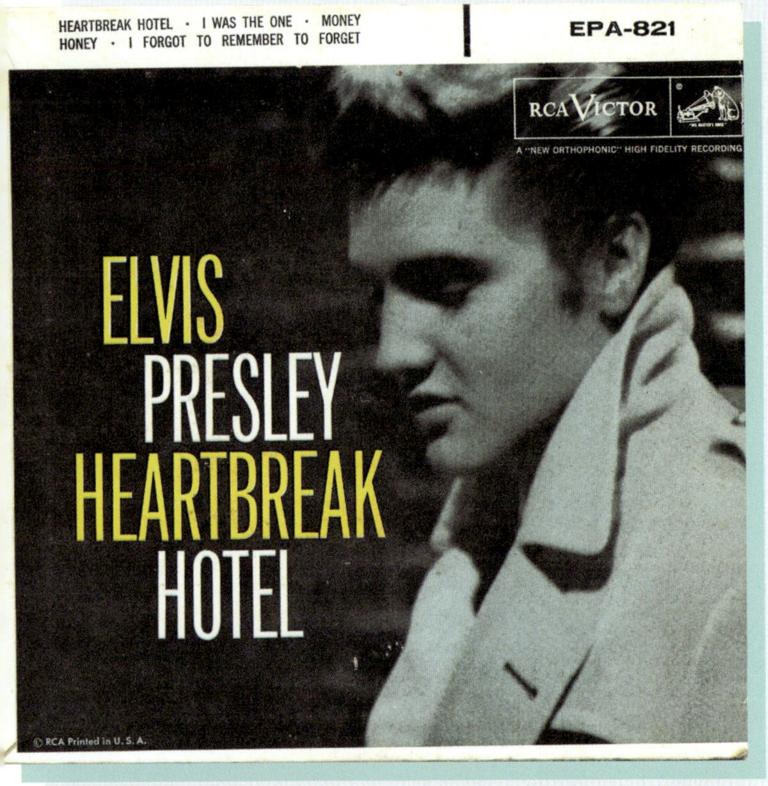

ABOVE: Heartbreak Hotel single
RIGHT: Elvis shows his trademark wiggling in Jailhouse Rock

Legend goes that its lyrics about alienation and rejection had been inspired by a newspaper article about the suicide of a young man who jumped from a hotel window.

Elvis however saw something in the song and chose it as his first RCA single. It was released on 27 January 1956 and Elvis sang it live when he made his first networked television appearance on *Stage Show* that same month.

The increasing popularity of TV during the 1950s was perfectly timed for the rise of Elvis and he made several appearances during early 1956. Propelled by such national exposure, Elvis got his breakthrough with *Heartbreak Hotel*, his first #1 single and first million-seller, which topped the Billboard 100 chart for seven weeks, the Cashbox singles chart for six weeks and the Country and Western Chart for 17 weeks. It also made number three on the R&B chart.

Paul McCartney said of the song; 'His phrasing, his use of echo, it's all so beautiful, as if he's singing it from the depths of hell'. Teenagers related and Elvis moved from being a regional celebrity to the national stage.

As well as making Elvis famous, the song made an incredible impact on many of the mega-star musicians who would follow in his wake, including The Beatles. Paul McCartney described the recording as nothing less than the most important artistic creation of the modern era, while John Lennon famously mooted the thought that; "Without Elvis, there would be no Beatles".

He stood out not just because of his new sound, but also by being so completely different to any of his predecessors in the way he performed on stage.

His trademark wiggling, quivering, shaking and pelvis-thrusting style earned him the nickname 'Elvis the Pelvis' and led to outrage and controversy as some journalists and older viewers considered his gyrating hips to be improper, even obscene. This led to his sometimes being filmed for television from the waist up. But in concert no such censoring was possible!

Elvis's nationally networked television appearances helped him build on his recording success – and he proved a natural performer. The camera loved him. His talent and voice, combined with good looks, sex appeal

6240

62

62

ABOVE: Elvis Presley promoting the movie Love Me Tender directed by Robert D. Webb

RIGHT: Original Jailhouse Rock poster

and electrifying, energetic and unconfined performances brought him phenomenal fame and attention.

Elvis was central to the birth of rock and roll and the kids loved it – although their parents, used to the rather calmer, crooning performances of singers such as Bing Crosby and Frank Sinatra, were appalled. While he was incredibly popular with his teenage fanbase, he was not a hit with older audiences and religious groups. But if anything, their disdain for him just fuelled his new-found celebrity.

In 1956 Elvis added 'movie star' to his list of career achievements, filming the huge hit 'Love Me Tender', which he followed up with 'Jailhouse Rock' and 'King Creole', before undertaking his national service in Germany.

NATIONAL SERVICE

After winning the Second World War, America and the UK maintained major military commitments abroad, not least in occupying post-war Germany and Japan. It was also a time of tension in the Cold War between the US and the Soviet Union. To help meet these various needs for increased manpower, the wartime conscription was extended into an obligatory period of National Service for men of military age.

In the UK, the National Service Act came into force in 1949 and required all physically fit men aged between 17 and 21 to serve 18 months in one of the armed forces.

America's system of military conscription, known as 'the draft', ran with varying criteria between 1940 to 1973. By the largely peaceful period of the late 1950s and early 1960s it needed fewer conscripts, but all healthy young men aged between 17-21 were obliged to serve in the country's armed services for 18 months.

The most famous conscript of all joined the ranks of the military in 1958 in the shape of GI Elvis Presley. He was posted to West Germany where his duties were less than arduous, usually involving driving more senior officers around. He even had time to sign autographs for fans in his lunch hour. To be fair, Elvis could probably have escaped the draft altogether after being offered several special roles in recognition of his unusual status as soldier/superstar, including the chance simply to entertain the troops. But a patriotic Elvis turned down all such suggestions, preferring to serve as a regular soldier in the army. His manager Colonel Parker also reckoned that any perception of bending the rules would be bad for business, whereas a stint in the military could help Elvis win over the older generations and overcome the slew of negative headlines which swirled around him then.

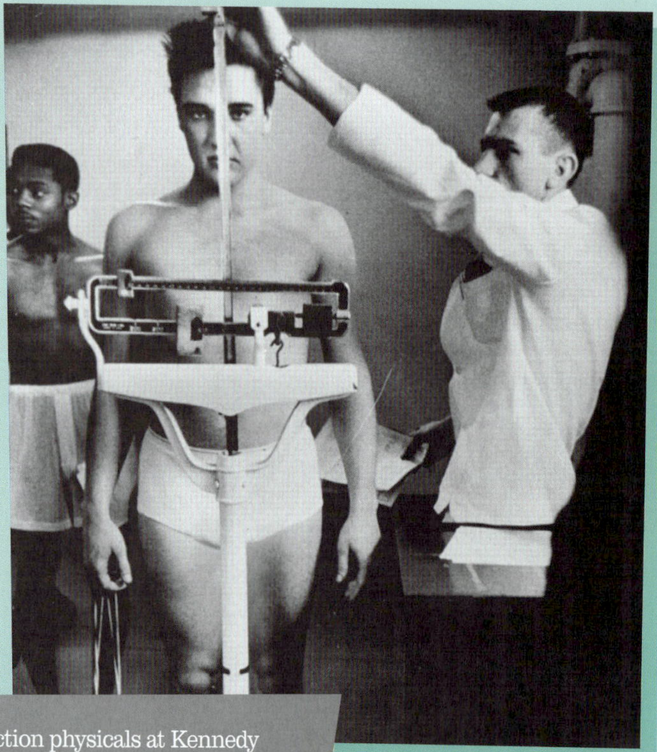

ABOVE: Elvis Presley's pre-induction physicals at Kennedy Veterans Hospital, 1958

HELL ON

BELOW & BOTTOM LEFT: Elvis performing at his '68 Comeback Special

BOTTOM RIGHT: Elvis in Las Vegas during a concert, December 1975

By the time Elvis returned to America in 1960 the rock and roll baton was being carried by others. Elvis went back to the studio and although he would make two dozen more movies and enjoy more hit singles and albums, the huge excitement around his early career was overtaken by his icon status which positioned him more at the middle of the road.

By 1965 Elvis had gone two years without a top ten hit song. The rock and pop music he had inspired had overtaken him, leaving him apparently out of touch and out of date. Even RCA realised something had to be done before their star turn was buried under the weight and quality of work coming from British bands such as The Beatles and The Rolling Stones. So, in what turned out to be a great idea, they unearthed an old recording they had previously shelved. This was *Crying in The Chapel,* which confounding all expectations, made number one in the UK and number three in the US giving his musical career a welcome boost. He wouldn't have another top 10 hit until 1968.

Seeming to accept that his rock and roll days were over, Elvis reinvented himself as a balladeer targeting a more mature audience. He went for a richer, fuller sound during the 1970s, using strong vibrato and adding a gospel flavour to his performances.

His rapport with audiences remained strong and he often reminisced about the early days. Altogether he played more than 700 performances in Las Vegas between 1969 and 1976.

Such was the impact of Elvis Presley that even today, years after his untimely death from a heart attack on 16 August 1977 aged just 42, he remains the best-selling solo artist in the history of recorded music by record sales, many of them notched up after his death.
The extraordinary facts of his life are simply that Elvis, born poor and with no connections, died in a mansion on a street named in his honour, as a cultural phenomenon, having changed the course of popular music for ever.

CHAPTER SIX

Get Your Kicks

IN 1956

1956 was the year rock and roll exploded into the mainstream. Powered by the popularity of Elvis Presley, rock and roll became an international phenomenon. As the Rolling Stone's Keith Richards puts it 'Elvis had hit like a bombshell. It was like the world went from black and white to Technicolor'.

After *Heartbreak Hotel*, Elvis's other major hit single in 1956 was the double A-side *Don't Be Cruel /Hound Dog* which between them topped the American pop charts for 11 weeks – a record that stood for 36 years – while also simultaneously making #1 on the US country and R&B charts. By 1958 the single had become only the third song in history to sell more than three million copies, after Bing Crosby's *White Christmas* and Gene Autry's *Rudolph the Red-Nosed Reindeer*. It is Elvis' best-selling song of all.

Elvis's early television appearances saw him singing and doing sketches on popular shows including The Dorsey Brothers Stage Show, The Milton Berle Show, The Steve Allen Show and The Ed Sullivan Show.

RIGHT: Ed Sullivan
ABOVE RIGHT: Elvis and Ed Sullivan in NY City, October 26, 1956
FAR RIGHT: Steve Allen

American television was enjoying a 'golden age' when many shows were performed live. In 1956 Ed Sullivan, in particular, was immensely popular and anyone who was anyone in entertainment featured on his show, which was usually broadcast live from New York. Sullivan was something of a broadcasting pioneer who introduced many new acts across all branches of entertainment, from comedians to old vaudeville acts, and including musicians. He was quick to see the appeal of the new rock and roll and is credited with broadcasting the first rock and roll song on national television when Bill Haley and His Comets performed *Rock Around the Clock* in August 1955.

But Sullivan had always drawn the line at having Elvis on his show, saying that he 'wouldn't consider' presenting him before his family audience.

So when Elvis got the call to appear on the 9 September 1956 episode of the show it was a shock. The simple explanation for the change of heart was that Sullivan needed to boost his programme having been trounced in the ratings by his fierce rival Steve Allen when he hosted Elvis a few weeks before.

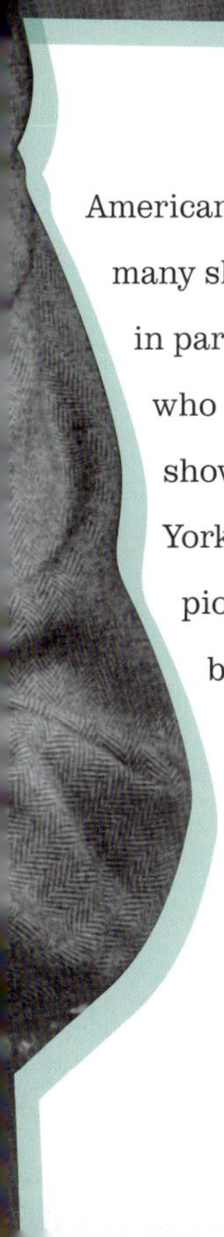

The change of mind was a sound decision as The Ed Sullivan Show that night attracted 60,710,000 viewers, one of the largest in US television history. Elvis would make two further appearances on the show, in October 1956 and January 1957 - the latter of which has become famous for only showing Elvis from the waist up. By the time of his last appearance on the show, Elvis would have broken the record for the highest number of concurrent singles by an individual artist by taking nine of the positions on the Billboard Top 100. He would make very few TV appearances ever again in his career, having become too big for the small screen with such unprecedented stardom. Elvis also found that his concerts became unmanageable because of the incredible reaction from fans who responded to the expression and emotion of his performances. His original band broke up and, in search of some privacy he retreated with his family behind the gates of his newly purchased home, Graceland. He had signed a huge movie deal with Paramount and by the end of 1956 his big screen feature debut Love Me Tender was among the top 10 biggest grossing films of that year.

The movie industry was quick to seize on the popularity of rock and roll and in 1956 many popular singers of the time, including Chuck Berry, appeared in Rock, Rock, Rock – an early jukebox musical. This film also featured DJ Alan Freed playing himself.

Although Freed's career ended somewhat ignominiously when he was accused of having played certain records for money, his contribution to the success of rock and roll has since been re-recognised and he was inducted into the Radio Hall of Fame in 1988.

But despite the huge impact of television and the big screen in popularising rock and roll, it was radio which continued to cater for the most committed fans. CBS Radio premiered its 'Rock 'n' roll Dance Party' in 1956, also hosted by Alan Freed, which went to become the first ever, regular, nationally broadcast rock and roll show.

ABOVE: Original Rock, Rock, Rock film poster

Left: Elvis strolls the grounds of his Graceland estate, circa 1957

CHAPTER SEVEN

A Whole Lotta
SHAKIN' GOIN' ON
1957

Seeing the impact of rock and roll in culture, TV stations were quick to cash in on the possibilities.

Dick Clark would make further inroads into bringing rock and roll to the nation's living rooms the following year when his Philadelphia local music and dance programme 'Bandstand' went national as 'American Bandstand'. First broadcast nationally on 5 August 1957, the show allowed teenagers to check out the latest acts and copy the dance moves. Dick Clark's clean-cut persona and natural presenting style helped to make rock and roll less threatening and more palatable to mainstream audiences. It was a perfectly timed melding of television, as the increasingly dominant media, and rock and roll as the all-conquering popular music style.

The show aired every day at 3 to 4.40pm and soon began attracting audiences of some 20 million - not just teenagers watching after school, but also their parents. Similar local afternoon shows sprang up all around the country. Budget and sets were generally meagre, but the music did the heavy lifting. American Bandstand also inspired Top of the Pops in the UK.

As well as showing its teenage studio audience dancing live to hit music from the Top 40, the programme would feature one act who would lip-sync to their current song and answer a few questions from Dick Clark. In August 1957, the American Bandstand featured act was one Jerry Lee Lewis who performed his hit *Whole Lotta Shakin' Goin' On* – his second single and the track which propelled him to international fame.

Another pioneer of rockabilly and rock and roll, Jerry Lee

ABOVE: Jerry Lee Lewis on the Steve Allen Plymouth Show in 1957

Left: Dick Clark

Jerry Lee Lewis

American singer, songwriter and pianist

1935 - 2022

'He could tear an audience apart'

Hank Williams Jr.

Audacious and arrogant, rollicking and rowdy, Jerry Lee Lewis took spontaneity to the brink of danger. With his wild eyes and sometimes shocking behaviour, he personified early 50s rock and roll at its best.

Signed by Sun Records to replace its star Elvis Presley after they sold him to RCA, Jerry Lee Lewis had a massive hit with his second single *Whole Lotta Shakin' Goin' On* in April 1957, which made him internationally famous. The song had been around for a few years, but no other recordings quite cut through.

However, having become a mainstay of his live sets where it was always rapturously received by audiences, it eventually became a hit when Jerry performed it on television. Following appearances on the massively popular Steve Allen show, Jerry's version went on to sell more than six million copies, reaching #3 in the US and #8 in the UK.

His biggest American chart hit came six months later in November with the rock and roll classic *Great Balls of Fire*. It just missed out on a US #1, held back #2 by *At the Hop* by Danny and the Juniors but was #1 for two weeks in the UK. Its 'Goodness gracious, great balls of fire ...' line and accompanying glissando, remains one of the most recognisable sections of popular music.

Like Little Richard before him, Jerry Lee Lewis treated the piano not only as an instrument, but also as a prop. His poor family had mortgaged their farm in order to buy him his first piano, and he learned from playing with his cousins. His style was similar to Little Richard's, but included elements of country piano. One of his early influences was country boogie player Moon Mullican, whose piano style was a precursor to rock and roll. Lewis developed his style at a young age, transforming traditional gospel numbers into boogie songs to the dismay of his local church leaders.

On stage he would play standing up, having kicked the seat out from under him. He danced on top of the piano while the band continued to play. His influence was clear to see 25 years later in the more mainstream performances of Elton John and Billy Joel.

But his time as a leading rock and roller was brief, blown up by a sexual scandal when he made the career-ending move of marrying his 13-year-old first cousin.

After laying low for a while he made his comeback on the country music scene where he became a top-selling artist once again. He was one of the first people inducted in the Rock and Roll Hall of Fame (in 1986) an achievement he followed up by being inducted into the Country Hall of Fame in 2022.

Listen to:

High School Confidential

Whole Lotta Shakin' Goin On

Chantilly Lace

Great Balls of Fire

ABOVE & RIGHT: Jerry Lee Lewis concert posters

TOWER
BALLROOM
BOB WOOLER
Presents
THUR, MAY, 17
7.30 P.M.
THANK YOUR LUCKY STARS SHOW
Jerry Lee Lewis
11 STAR GROUPS
Local Press for Details
Usual Agencies
TICKETS.. 5/- ADVANCE, 6/6 at DOOR

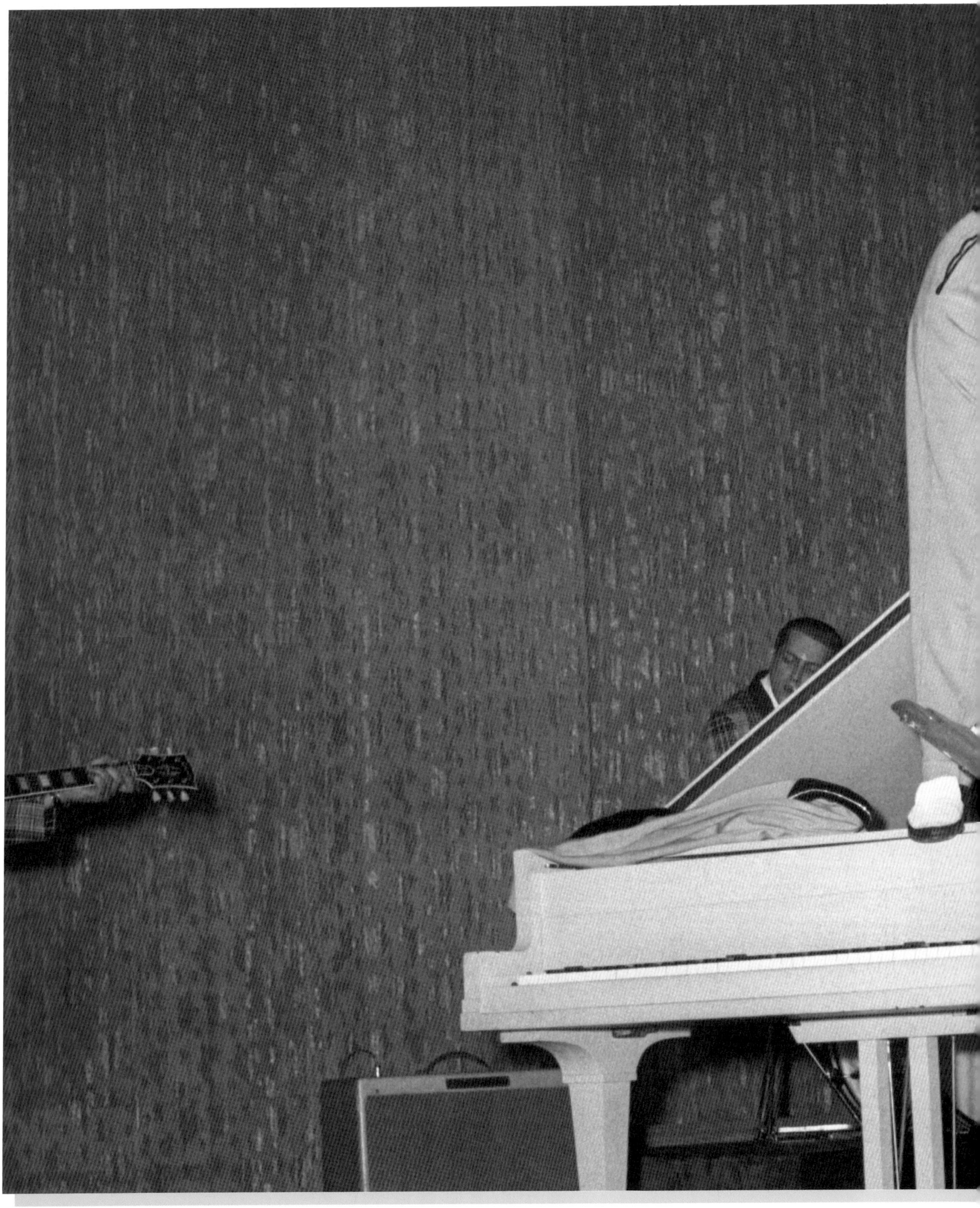

ABOVE: Jerry Lee Lewis gives an enthusiastic performance at the Cafe de Paris in New York City on June 10, 1958

ABOVE: Jerry Lee Lewis, Carl Perkins, Elvis Presley and Johnny Cash as "The Million Dollar Quartet" Dec 4, 1956, Memphis, Tennessee

TOP RIGHT: Danny & The Juniors *At The Hop*

RIGHT: Gene Vincent

Lewis was a dynamic musician who gave crazy and wild performances which earned him the nickname 'the killer'. His first billing was as 'Jerry Lee Lewis and his Pumping Piano'.

The self-taught singer and instrumentalist was second only to Elvis in terms of being a white man able to make a meaningful fist of R&B and translate that into arresting rock and roll numbers. His main instrument was piano which he commanded to perfection, as evidenced by his most famous hit, the classic *Great Balls of Fire,* released in November 1957. Like Elvis, he was among the alumni of Sam Phillip's Sun Records where he worked initially as a session musician until he began to make his own hit music. During his time at Sun he was part of the impromptu jam session with Elvis, Carl Perkins and Johnny Cash in December 1956, which came to be known as the Million Dollar Quartet.

While Jerry was already a star by the time of his Bandstand performances, the show gave some acts their big break. In 1957 for example, Danny & The Juniors

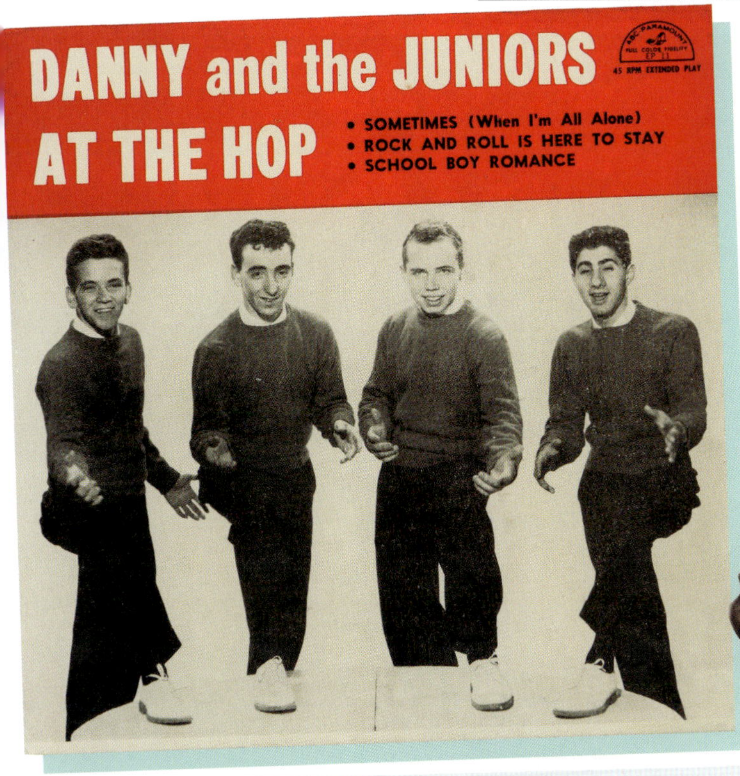

came to national notice shortly after their appearance in early December singing *At the Hop,* which went on to top the charts within weeks.

Another act breaking through in the mid-1950s was Gene Vincent, who enjoyed a handful of Top 40 hits in the US between 1956 and 1957, the most enduring of which is the rockabilly-style *Be-Bop-A Lula*.

Born Vincent Eugene Craddock, he was signed by Capitol Records as their answer to Elvis Presley. It proved to be a sound investment when *Be-Bop-A-Lula*, his debut single, became a huge hit. The song has since been covered many times by artists including the Everly Brothers, and Beatles John Lennon and (separately) Paul McCartney.

Speaking on the 400th episode of the legendary BBC music programme Desert Island Discs in 1982, Paul McCartney told presenter Roy Plomley that Gene Vincent's *Be-Bop-A-Lula* had made a big impression on him and was the first single he ever bought. He added that rock and roll was the kind of music that 'just sent tingles up your spine, to me [rock 'n' roll] seemed like a whole new direction of music... All these people in crazy clothes with guitars and stuff and slicked-back hair'.

and his
BLUE CAPS

For the record, Paul's other selections included Elvis Presley's *Heartbreak Hotel*, Chuck Berry's *Sweet Little Sixteen*, and Little Richard's *Tutti Frutti, while* his luxury item was a guitar - make unspecified.

But although Gene Vincent inspired a young Paul McCartney and attracted a huge cult following, he didn't come to rival Elvis in the longer term. He went on to have more success in the UK than in his native America and continued performing throughout the 1960s. Famously, he was touring the UK in 1960 with fellow rocker Eddie Cochran when the two men were involved in a car crash. While Gene was thrown clear and escaped with broken bones, Eddie was killed. Although Gene was lucky on that night, it only bought him another decade or so as he died in 1971 aged just 36 from an ulcer and other complications after years of health problems and related medication, coupled with other drug and alcohol dependencies.

The other big star who broke through in 1957 was singer/songwriter Buddy Holly and his band The Crickets. Buddy was a central figure in the development of mid-50s rock and roll. He had a distinctive vocal style incorporating little hiccoughs and falsetto, which he used to full effect on his biggest hits, the classics *That'll Be the Day* and *Peggy Sue.*

LEFT: Gene Vincent and His Blue Caps perform on the set of the movie "The Girl Can't Help It" in 1956 in Los Angeles, California

FAR LEFT: Eddie Cochran

ABOVE & RIGHT: Gene Vincent adverts from the late 1950s

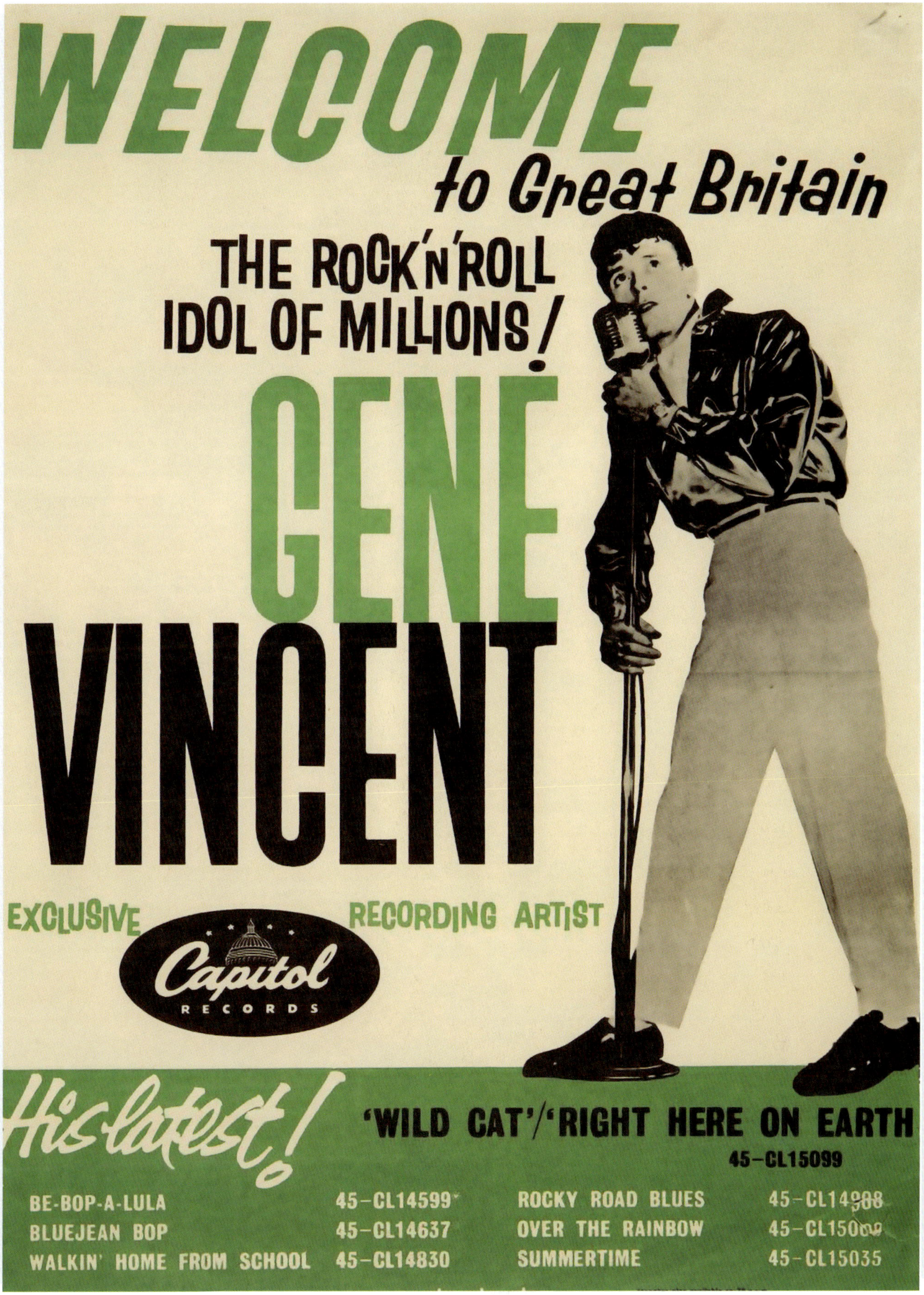
WELCOME
to Great Britain
THE ROCK'N'ROLL IDOL OF MILLIONS!
GENE VINCENT
EXCLUSIVE RECORDING ARTIST
Capitol RECORDS
His latest!
'WILD CAT'/'RIGHT HERE ON EARTH
45-CL15099
BE-BOP-A-LULA 45-CL14599
BLUEJEAN BOP 45-CL14637
WALKIN' HOME FROM SCHOOL 45-CL14830
ROCKY ROAD BLUES 45-CL14988
OVER THE RAINBOW 45-CL150
SUMMERTIME 45-CL15035

ABOVE: Portrait of Eddie Cochran

Buddy Holly

American singer/songwriter,

born Charles Hardin Holley

1936 - 1959

'I thought I'd died and gone to heaven ... it was like seeing an instrument from outer space and I said to myself: 'That's the future – that's what I want'

Eric Clapton on the first time he saw Holly and his Fender guitar

One of rock's first singer-songwriter-guitarists, Buddy Holly was a giant of rock and roll, whose distinctive and influential talent saw him enjoy a brief but dazzling career before his untimely death in a plane crash in 1959 aged just 22. His achievements are all the more incredible in light of his youth.

Having learned to play guitar while growing up in a musical family in Lubbock in Texas, Buddy was influenced by gospel, country and R&B acts of the 1940s when he began performing with his friends from high school. He made his first appearance on local television in 1952 and went on to open for Elvis Presley several times, working with his friend Bob Montgomery as 'Buddy and Bob'.

The 'e' was dropped from his surname, accidentally on his first record contract and Buddy decided to stick with it.

In 1955, inspired by Elvis, his style shifted too – away from country to rock and roll - and he was signed by Decca Records. But, unhappy with some of the restrictions as he tried to move away from the country sound Decca liked, Buddy moved to work closer to his Texas home with producer Norman Petty in Clovis, New Mexico. It was after this that the big hits started to flow. With his backing band (Niki Sullivan on second guitar and background vocals, Joe B. Mauldin on bass, and Jerry Allison on drums) now re-named as The Crickets, Buddy enjoyed his first big hit in September 1957, when the peppy *That'll Be the Day* topped the American and British singles charts.

Buddy wrote the breakthrough hit, with his great friend and collaborator Jerry Allison, after the pair had watched the Western movie 'The Searchers', which features the star actor John Wayne saying the line throughout the film.

This was followed in October by another major hit, *Peggy Sue.* The song had begun life as *Cindy Lou* named after Buddy's niece. But Jerry persuaded him to rejig it as Peggy Sue in honour of his then girlfriend and future wife Peggy Sue Gerron.

Their first album *The Chirping Crickets* was released in November 1957 and reached #5 in the UK. Together with producer Norman Petty, Buddy's tracks became famous for featuring imaginative effects such as echo chambers and overdubbing, which superimposed one recording on another.

Following successful tours of the US, UK and Australia and 1958 hit albums *Buddy Holly and That'll Be the Day*, things changed for Buddy in late 1958. He had got married and moved to New York with his new wife María Elena. The Crickets preferred to stay in Texas, so the group separated. But the main problem was that there wasn't much money for any of them; despite the fame and success they had enjoyed, Buddy and the band were receiving very little in royalties.

So, broke and a bit disillusioned, Buddy took a job on a gruelling tour of the American mid-west. It was to prove a fatal decision.

During this tour Buddy was killed in a plane crash, along with two of his fellow performers, 17-year-old Ritchie Valens and 28-year-old Jiles (JP) Richardson, known professionally as The Big Bopper. The date was 3 February 1959 and – with all three dying way before their time - the tragedy which came to be known as 'The Day the Music Died' after Don McLean immortalised the accident in his 1971 smash hit song *American Pie.*

Buddy had been so prolific during his tragically short career that many recordings were found and released posthumously.

He is considered responsible for launching the 'two guitars, bass and drums' combo which went on to be so common in modern-era rock and roll bands. British band the Hollies reportedly named themselves after him as a tribute, and artists such as Bob Dylan, Eric Clapton and the Beatles have mentioned Buddy as a major influence. He was among the first artists inducted into the Rock and Roll Hall of Fame in 1986, shortly after it was established, and is ranked at 13 in Rolling Stone magazine's list of 100 Greatest Artists.

By now the throbbing beat from the US could not be ignored and the UK began to develop its own answer to what was happening across the Atlantic. Here too, and for the first time, teenagers were a cohesive and separate economic group looking for something to attach themselves too – rock and roll proved to be the answer.

Listen to:

That'll Be The Day

Peggy Sue

True Love Ways

Not Fade Away

Oh, Boy!

ABOVE: Buddy Holly and The Crickets perform on Ed Sullivan's CBS variety show 'Toast of the Town,' New York, December 1, 1957

CHAPTER EIGHT

Rock and Roll IN THE UK

British rock and roll was a strange beast which existed only briefly.

As Britain began to recover from the deprivation and devastation of the Second World War, the country's teenagers found themselves looking across the Atlantic for hope and inspiration. When they discovered American rock and roll they were immediately enthralled and wanted a piece of the action for themselves. Immediately before the advent of rock and roll, British kids had congregated around skiffle music – another American export born from ragtime jazz and blues-influenced folk music from New Orleans. It had sprung up among 'poor' musicians using whatever they could get their hands on as percussive instruments. Originally this could have been as rudimentary as a kazoo or a comb and paper, but came on to include bathtubs, tea chests and, famously, washboards, which could be tapped or scraped to knock out a pleasing tune, if a little raw, underproduced and rough around the edges.

Although it had been around for a while, in the early 1950s skiffle suddenly erupted in the UK like nowhere else as teenagers turned against the prevalent big swing band sound. Modern commentators have likened it to the advent of punk in the late 1970s – a reaction against the music business by taking things back to basics and giving a young generation something which its parents could never understand. Skiffle was wonderfully inclusive; acoustic and scrubby, allowing anyone to make music cheaply and easily. Aspiring musicians were quick to seize on its possibilities, and many went on to become huge stars, including Jimmy Page who would go on to lead Led Zeppelin, Brian Jones, founder of The Rolling Stones, and John Lennon and Paul McCartney, whose pre-Beatles band The Quarrymen was a skiffle outfit, including a washboard.

Picture Post, 29 May, 1954

THE TRUTH ABOUT THE 'TEDDY BOYS' AND THE TEDDY GIRLS

The 'Edwardians,' or 'Teddy Boys,' have been branded as hooligans, juvenile gangsters and delinquents. They have also been called dandies and mother's darlings. It is a confusing picture of exaggeration and distortion. A PICTURE POST *investigation seeks to bring it into focus. Our staff writer, HILDE MARCHANT, presents the facts. A PSYCHIATRIST of much experience with young people, interprets them. JOSEPH McKEOWN took the pictures*

WE were in a dance-hall in Tottenham—a suburb of London—and the young men we wished to contact were distinctive and obvious. The floppy jackets hung to their knees, the poplin shirts were advertisement white, the trousers were ankle tight, the shoes were good black leather, and the ties were narrow bows. An ugly outfit? That is a matter of opinion; and we were not seeking opinion—only facts. To approach the facts meant we had first to approach the boys, talk to them, and challenge the honesty of their talk. And the first thing that struck me was that their clothes are deceptive. This Edwardian fashion gives a uniformity to a group of young people who are far from uniform. They are as varied, diverse and informal as any other group of human beings. They set a pattern in their velvet collars, dog-tooth checks and moccasin shoes. But there is no such standard pattern about their lives or behaviour.

But let them talk for themselves, for they are frank enough. What do they do during the day, or the week? One is a toy maker, one a glass cutter. Another is an engineer's apprentice, one a die cutter, another an electric welder and, surprisingly, another a National Serviceman on leave—back in his Teddy Boy civilian 'uniform.' (His hair was shorter than the others, but would still have horrified the Sergeant-major.) Their wages were good—ranging from the £4 17s. 6d. a week apprentice, to just over £12 a week for the skilled cabinet maker. Their suits cost between £17 and £20. All of them agreed that a good poplin shirt was just under £2 and that a pair of shoes was around the £3 mark. Most of them 'kept themselves'; which means they pay their parents something towards the rent and the household budget. Even so, pocket money was never less than £2 a week, and often double. They were not interested in drink—a beer, perhaps, but more likely a mineral water. They

THE SUIT THAT GRANDFATHER MIGHT HAVE WORN

The dance is contemporary jive. But the suit is an adaptation of the Edwardian 'masher's' outfit. It is also English in conception and, unlike recent men's fashions, owes nothing to Hollywood.

Lonnie Donegan

British skiffle musician and songwriter

born Anthony James Donegan

1931 - 2002

'.. he was the first person we had heard of from Britain to get to the coveted #1... he was the man'

Paul McCartney

One of Skiffle's biggest stars was the influential Lonnie Donegan, whose energetic style brought him an amazing run of hit singles in the UK between 1956 and 1962 including three #1s. One of his most successful records was *Rock Island Line*, which, in a case of pleasing circularity, had been written by the great black American folksinger Huddie Ledbetter, who had become famous as 'Lead Belly', in the 1930s. Lonnie Donegan's uptempo cover was a sensation, selling more than a million copies and becoming one of the first British pop records to break into the American Top 10. Following it up with a second American hit, *Does Your Chewing Gum Lose Its Flavour,* Lonnie became the first British male artist with two US Top 10 hits. Paul McCartney described Lonnie as '... the first person we had heard of from Britain to get to the coveted No. 1 in the charts, and we studied his records avidly. We all bought guitars to be in a skiffle group. He was the man.' Ironically it was the success of Paul McCartney and The Beatles in winning the chart battle overall which delivered a knockout blow to British Skiffle.

More mainstream instruments took centre stage as the genre evolved, including a mix from guitar, harmonica, piano accordion, double bass, banjo and mandolin. By 1957 there were more than 30,000 skiffle groups in Britain. But even they were no defence against the strength of the wave of rock and roll which hit the UK via cinema screens showing Blackboard Jungle with its Bill Haley *Rock Around the Clock* soundtrack. Again it brought incidents like those which caused problems in the US, with fans up on their feet, sometimes harmlessly dancing in the aisles, but also sometimes rioting. This corresponding mayhem in the UK was often down to Teddy Boys – the UK's first youth 'cult'.

Dressed in an unofficial uniform of drainpipe trousers, drape coats and 'brothel creeper' or 'beetle-crusher' thick, crepe-soled shoes, Teddy Boys would top off their look with a trademark slicked-back hairstyle, quiffed at the front and parted centrally down the back of the head and known as a duck's tail, or more colloquially as a DA. Their girlfriends would wear smart dresses or pencil shirts, with stockings, high heels and often have their hair piled on top of their heads in a style known as a 'beehive'.

While American teenagers had their drugstores and soda fountains, British youth socialised in coffee bars which became important centres for music.

Although originally associated with the British skiffle scene, the UK's coffee bars took centre stage as the country witnessed the strange alchemy of its ramshackle skiffle sound morphing into rock and roll. Teddy Boys adopted the new music as their own, listening to American artists such as Elvis Presley, Eddie Cochran, and Bill Haley.

BELOW: A 'Teddy Boy' in a London street, 29th May 1954

LONDON TRANSPORT
BALHAM SUBSTATION
214 LEONARDS
(CAR HIRE) LTD
Leonards CARS

With their warm interiors furnished with colourful jukeboxes and noisy Italian espresso machines, coffee bars offered teenagers reasonably cheap access to an exotic seeming sanctuary, quite different from anything else on offer on the drab post-war city streets. Sometimes they would even host live performances. One of the most famous was '2is' which opened on Old Compton Street in 1956. With just a small stage in its basement, built from bits of wood and milk crates, '2is' hosted sets from British talents including Tommy Steele, Cliff Richard, Hank Marvin, Adam Faith, Marty Wilde, and Joe Brown. These artists all played to a maximum crowd of around 20 people and were backed by an array of talented musicians perfecting their musicianship and who would all go on to enjoy successful musical careers for years to come.

2is became a pioneering venue for British rock and roll and remained key to the genre's success, prior to the emergence of the 'Mersey sound' from Liverpool in the early 1960s. Having closed in 1970, its location is now marked by a plaque describing it as the 'birthplace of British rock and roll and the popular music industry'.

Although they lapped up American music, most British rock and roll fans would have found it impossible to make the trip across the Atlantic to see and hear their idols in person. For the average British teenager in the late 50s, although they suddenly found themselves with some disposable income, a trip to America was about as likely as a trip to Mars.

LEFT: A group of Teddy Boys arriving at South Western Court to face charges of insulting behaviour and carrying offensive weapons on Tooting Bec Common, June 1956.

Union issues meant it was difficult for the American stars to travel to perform in the UK. So the success and proliferation of early rock and roll was entirely dependent on radio and records. There was a real need for some

homegrown talent and plenty of aspiring British musicians keen to take the opportunity. The honour of becoming the UK's first rock and roll star went to Tommy Steele, who, presented as the UK's answer to Elvis, became a pin up pop star and recorded hit singles including *Rock with The Caveman* in 1956 and *Singing the Blues* in 1957.

Another artist first mooted as the 'English Elvis' was Cliff Richard, who delivered his 1958 guitar track *Move It!,* with snarling conviction, smouldering looks to camera, curling lips and swivelling hips. *Move It* is considered as the first authentic British rock and roll record and credited with laying the foundations for the Beatles and the Merseybeat sound. John Lennon reportedly said that 'there had been nothing worth listening to in British music pre-Cliff'. But even so, Cliff and his contemporaries

LEFT: Tommy Steele
ABOVE: *Move It* 7" by Cliff Richard
RIGHT: Cliff Richard in the late 50s

couldn't crack the American charts as British rock and roll remained in the shadows of the original.

Undeterred, and boosted by an appearance on the popular TV music show 'Oh Boy!', Cliff took the opportunity to emulate Elvis even further by following his move from stage to screen. In the early 1960s Cliff enjoyed a thriving career as a film star with hits including *The Young Ones* and *Summer Holiday*.

In 1956 the import ban on jukeboxes was lifted and so they began to arrive in the UK to play their part in the coffee bar boom – within two years the UK was home to 8,000 jukeboxes. As rock and roll elevated the status of the jukebox, the industry boomed. Bearing the logos of their famous makers, Wurlitzer and Rock-Ola, jukeboxes livened up many a suburban café with their cool designs featuring chrome grills and tail fins to mimic flash cars of the time.

But where rock and roll was concerned there was controversy at every turn. Even coffee bars and jukeboxes were derided as the older generation thought them a terrific way for young people to waste their time. As the Lord Mayor of Birmingham put it in 1958, 'I do not think it a proper thing for groups of young people to go into coffee bars and spend hour after hour listening to records, buying cups of tea and coffee and bottles of pop...... feeding pennies into jukeboxes and fruit machines because they had nothing better to do with their spare time'.

Homegrown talent aside, UK fans did have one treat in the form of a visit from American rock and roll superstar Bill Haley who arrived to tour the UK on 5 February 1957. Imagine the excitement at his arrival - he was the real deal, despite his unlikely 'un-pop-star-like' looks.

Bill Haley and his entourage travelled from America on the Queen Mary liner, disembarking at Southampton to board a chartered train branded the 'Bill Haley Rock 'n' Roll Special'. As it sped to London the train was cheered along the route by people precariously balanced

on bridges and embankments. On arrival at Waterloo Station, Bill and the band were mobbed by an estimated 4,000 fans, delaying their departure to their hotel in a chauffeur-driven Rolls Royce. Similar scenes greeted his first concert when the tour kicked off at the Dominion in London. It was an overwhelming triumph as song after song, from *Razzle Dazzle* to *Shake Rattle and Roll,* as well as *Rock Around the Clock* of course, was greeted with deafening roars of approval. It was the same story as Bill travelled the country on his 30-date tour.

He and the Comets toured Australia that same year and then returned to Europe in 1958 for a successful (if riot-dominated) tour of the mainland. Bill Haley and His Comets were the first major American rock and roll act to tour the world in this way. Elvis never toured outside America, save a few trips over the border to Canada in the mid-1950s. Had he done so he would have attracted huge audiences and made his overseas fans very happy. Considering that a world tour would also have made mountains of cash and his manager Colonel Parker was a marketing genius all about the bottom line it's strange that Parker wouldn't have set this up.

So there had to be another reason. There was. Parker was an illegal immigrant with no passport. And he couldn't risk getting one for fear his secret would come out. So he would regularly thwart any thoughts about touring from Elvis and quash any offers from overseas with warnings about 'security issues' were Elvis to leave the United States.

RIGHT: Bill Haley And His Comets, rehearsing 'Rock Around the Clock' in London for their first British performance

One other popular, but mainstream, singer who did visit the UK in the mid-1950s was Rosemary Clooney, whose hits included *Come On-a My House* and *Mambo Italiano*. During a series of appearances in the UK in 1955, Rosemary declared that she would never record rock and roll. 'Where's the story value in those songs? I feel that every good song should tell a story', she said, adding, '... Those sax players, for instance, they don't tune up from year to year, let along from day to day, and the singers just have no respect for the basic do-re-mi!'

Television executives of the time evidently disagreed with Rosemary and instead were quick to pick up on the fact that rock and roll was here to stay. UK television executives made dedicated programmes including the BBC's *Six-Five Special* which began in February 1957, running at 6pm every Saturday night, aimed at the 16-25 age group. In November that year the show was broadcast from the stage in the 2i's basement.

Commercial television also picked up on the idea and broadcast their rock and roll offering 'Oh Boy' in 1958. Suddenly the hungry audiences were being served up the cream of rock and roll in their front rooms as television helped create the market and framework for British rock and roll to grow nationwide.

But in just a few short years the British rock and roll scene had calmed down considerably. Perhaps because American artists kept churning out such remarkable and unbeatable hits, the British imitative rock simply rolled over. Cliff Richard had abandoned his wannabe Elvis persona in favour of more middle of the road melodic music with his huge hit *Living Doll* and Tommy Steele had moved into musical films and theatre. Cliff and Tommy are both now British Knights of the Realm in recognition of their services to charity and entertainment respectively.

Cliff's backing band The Shadows, led by Hank Marvin, went on to have instrumental hits including *Apache* and *Dance On!* and are considered innovative and influential artists, among the most successful of the era.

In general, early British rock and roll was never much of a rival to the American original. By the early 1960s it had given way to the new wave of beat and R&B-based artists, notably Billy Fury, the Yardbirds and the Rolling Stones. But although its reign may have been brief, it was a necessary part of the evolution of rock and roll and instrumental in all music that would follow it.

By 1962 the sharp decline in British rock and roll was complete. Within 12 months the Beatles would come along, break America, shake up rock and roll and smash everything in their wake, including even the rock and roll version of Elvis.

ABOVE: On the set of Six-Five Special, Saturday 22nd February 1958
LEFT: Rosemary Clooney

CHAPTER NINE

The Sound Of

ROCK AND ROLL

As rock and roll came ahead of the advent of stereo recordings in the 1960s, the recording process for rock and roll was mono – using only one channel and then transmitting the same sound to all speakers.

What's All This Talk About HI-FI?

By Robert Gorman

THAT BIG SOUND sweeping the country is high fidelity—complete with words and music. The music is sweet when you hear it, but some of the words drown out the tune. Everywhere people are talking a gobbledegook language of decibels, intermodulation distortion, pickup compliance, woofers, tweeters, bass and treble boost.

One of the most startling developments in hi-fi

Lafayette Radio sketches
Electronic Workshop photo

This meant that, in essence, all the tracks were 'live recordings'; produced with everyone involved in one room at one time, with very limited possibilities for changing anything afterwards. If anyone made a mistake, everyone had to run through the whole song again, take after take, until it was right. The musicians were only as good as the performance they gave that day - there was no mixing process as we know it today as the technology just wasn't there.

Studio engineers, such as they existed, were expert in setting up and placing microphones to capture the sound on a simple mono (one-channel) machine. Stereo recordings didn't start to come in until the very late 1950s, developed in a quest to make a recording that could produce live sound more faithfully in a so-called 'high fidelity' (hi-fi) technology. Humans hear the world round them through two ears – and stereo more closely mimics this with some sound coming from the left speaker and some from the right.

But in the meantime it was down to the talents of early engineers and producers, such as Sam Phillips of Sun Records, to make rock and roll work in mono. Sam was a master of sound whose abilities with slap back echo

ABOVE: Jerry Lee Lewis with producer Sam Phillips at the Sun Studios in Memphis in 1958

LEFT: 1950s HI-FI advert

and tape delay are now legendary. Working out of a basic property incorporating a front office, a 20 x 35-foot live area and a tiny control room equipped with basic tape recorders, he had an instinct for getting the best out of the acoustics available.

'He was always trying to invent sound,' says Sam's son Jerry Phillips. 'He felt the studio was his laboratory.' In that vein, it's amusing to note that many sound engineers actually wore white coats in the 1950s.

The story goes that when Elvis left Sam to sign with RCA, recording staff there went to extraordinary lengths to try and mimic the sound of the old Sun recordings including standing in the corridors to get the echo. RCA and its engineers would go on to innovate and improve sound recording throughout the 1950s and 1960s so that the RCA studio become one of the most successful of all time and is credited with creating the famous Nashville sound.

Other famous studios were set up in old churches to take advantage of the acoustics there. Bill Haley and His Comets recorded *Rock Around the Clock* in the Pythian Temple in New York, where Decca had rented space and built a studio on the third floor to benefit from the brilliant acoustics offered by the building's high ceilings and wooden floors.

Improvements in technology meant that the old 78rpm records had made way for the increasingly popular, smaller, more cost-effective 45rpm format. Up to 100 records in 45rpm format would fit into one jukebox.

RIGHT: Two teenage girls in curlers dreamily listening to 45 RPM records on a vintage record player at home in the 1950s

TOP RIGHT: 1950s advert for portable 45rpm record player

WESTINGHOUSE
M-G-M
"Briefcase" Portable ... extra sensitive for use in every location. Operates on AC, DC, and long-life battery pack. Beautifully contrasted cabinets in Tan-and-Sand or Sand-and-Tan. Compact and lightweight. Less batteries ... $34.95. Model 575
45 RPM Record Player ... with built-in speaker for magnificent plug-in-and-play performance. Has tone control, micro-groove needle. Plays up to 50 minutes. So compact you can take it wherever you go. Needs no attachments. Only $39.95 Model 590
Radio and Television
NEW YORK 11, N. Y.
Emerson Radio and Television
REG. T. M.

ABOVE: A teenager waits to hear the latest recording at his local record shop, September 1956

RIGHT: A Radio Luxembourg annual from the 1950s

They were also more portable and therefore easier to sell in shops. Regular high street stores around the UK, including Boots the Chemist, W.H. Smith, and Woolworths, all found space on their shelves for the rock and roll records teenagers were buying at a giddying rate.

Records were so important because aside from coffee bars and jukeboxes, access to rock and roll music was otherwise difficult. Issues with music unions meant that in the UK the music was otherwise only available on radio from pirate station Radio Luxembourg. The BBC, still bound by its Reithian rules, had declared the new rock and roll music 'deplorable' and didn't play any of it. It had three main stations at the time, the Light Programme which featured music and light entertainment, comedy

and drama programmes; the Home Service, for news and features; and the Third Programme for classical music and educational lectures. Its principal aims were to 'inform, educate and entertain' ...but it didn't appear to angle any of those at teenage rock and roll fans.

Another technological advance which began to change the sound of rock and roll was in instruments. In early rock and roll music, the lead instruments were saxophones or piano, but by the middle and end of the 1950s, the guitar began to take centre stage.

Some guitar brands became almost as iconic as the artist who played them, for example Elvis Presley and Chuck Berry with their favoured Gibson acoustic guitars and Eddie Cochran and Gene Vincent with their Gretsch models.

The origins of the move to electric guitars a few years later are fuzzy. Although such instruments had been around in various forms for some years, the first mass produced electric guitars weren't around until the Broadcaster from Fender was launched in 1950. The name was short lived because of a trademark dispute with Gretsch, but the concept survived, and was renamed as the Telecaster which is still popular today having been through various incarnations over the past 70 years.

Fender went on to make the iconic Stratocaster, or 'Strat', which was the choice of Buddy Holly. His Sunburst Fender Stratocaster guitar is one of the most famous in rock and roll history and it was the instrument played during Buddy's final concert.....

LEFT: Maybellene, Chuck Berry's guitar, a Gibson ES-350T

ABOVE LEFT: Gretsch 6120 Chet Atkins hollow-body, used by Eddie Cochran

CHAPTER TEN

The Day THE MUSIC DIED

1959

Headliners Buddy Holly, Ritchie Valens and The Big Bopper played the Surf Ballroom in Clear Lake, Iowa, USA as part of their Winter Dance Party tour on 2 February 1959.

By this time Buddy had parted company with the Crickets who had wanted to stay in Texas after he moved to New York with his new wife María Elena. So he employed new backing musicians, including future country music star Waylon Jennings on bass, Tommy Allsup on guitar and Carl Bunch on drums.

Considering how famous those musicians were at the time, the amateurish nature of their tour arrangements seems incredible these days. Touring is always gruelling, but in the 1950s it was even more so. There was nothing like the entourages which support modern stars – 1950s musicians would do everything for themselves, from laundry to looking after their own instruments, including setting them up on stage as there weren't really any 'roadies' yet.

And of course, given the size of the USA there was a lot of ground to cover between the shows; often as many as 600 miles between each gig in a succession of one-night concerts.

While Buddy and his band were used to this, what they hadn't bargained for were the atrocious weather conditions in the mid-west of America that winter. During

ABOVE: Buddy Holly and Waylon Jennings photographed in a photo-booth in Central Station, in New York City, 1959

LEFT: Poster promoting the Winter Dance Party tour

what was the worst weather in the area for 30 years, the performers were travelling up to 500 miles between successive dates, criss-crossing the states of Minnesota, Wisconsin, and Iowa in the freezing cold each night. Even their tour buses were not up to scratch, frequently breaking down and often without working heaters. This was also before the days of super-highways interstate, so that the treacherous journeys were undertaken on two-lane country roads.

The weather was harsh, and everyone was cold and tired. One night when the tour bus broke down, it got so cold that drummer Carl Bunch sustained a case of frost bite so bad that he had to be hospitalised. The Big Bopper was coming down with flu. So that fateful night in February, Buddy had decided that rather than get back on the uncomfortable tour bus for the trip to the next stop of the tour in Minnesota, North Dakota, he would charter a plane, travel in comfort and arrive ahead of time. There was room for two other passengers, alongside Buddy and the pilot Roger Peterson, so two seats were offered around. Tommy Allsup tossed a coin with Ritchie Valens to see who would get the last seat on the plane. Ritchie won, exclaiming, "That's the first time I've won anything in my life!"

Bass player Waylon Jennings was in the running for the final seat. However, he kindly gave way and allowed the Bopper to take his place because he was suffering with flu.

That really was incredibly good luck for Tommy and Waylon, and awfully bad luck for Ritchie and the Bopper. Minutes after take-off the plane crashed, killing everyone on board outright.

Apparently the crash occurred because the pilot had not been informed of worsening weather conditions and was flying 'on instruments' meaning that he couldn't see the horizon.

RIGHT: The wreckage of the plane crash that killed rock stars Buddy Holly, Ritchie Valens, and The Big Bopper, on February 3, 1959, outside of Clear Lake, Iowa

LEFT: Waylon Jennings

N3794N

The Big Bopper

Born Jiles Perry 'JP' Richardson Jr

1930 - 1959

Vocalist The Big Bopper, named in honour of his imposing frame, was one of rock and roll's first 'novelty' artists, but also a true talent of rock and roll, rockabilly, and country genres. He began his career as a DJ and songwriter, before moving over to performance.

His 1958 hit *Chantilly Lace,* where the listener is privy to a risqué one-sided phone call, remains a classic of the era, made him a star and earned him a place on the Winter Dance Party tour with Buddy Holly and Ritchie Valens, where he closed the show. He was killed at 28 years of age alongside Buddy Holly and Ritchie Valens in a plane crash on February 3, 1959.

Ritchie Valens

Born Richard Valenzuela

1941 - 1959

'Talk about the Latin explosion – he's the one in charge'

Ricky Martin

Ritchie Valens was a famous Latino teen idol and pioneer of the Chicano rock movement of the 1950s and 60s. Signed to the Del-Fi label when he was aged just 16, Mexican-American Richard Valenzuela shortened his name to find fame as Ritchie Valens with his special take on rock and roll. Influenced by mariachi, flamenco and blues, Ritchie's big hit was 1958's *La Bamba*, previously a traditional Mexican folk song popular at weddings. Souped up rock and roll-style by Ritchie's wild guitar, it made the Billboard top 40 and the UK top 50 and made Ritchie the first Latino to cross over successfully to mainstream music, inspiring many artists, including Carlos Santana, since.

Sadly his career is measured in months - eight - following his death aged just 17 in the plane crash which also killed Buddy Holly and The Big Bopper in February 1959. He was posthumously inducted into the Rock and Roll Hall of Fame in 2001, the Grammy Hall of Fame in 2000 and given a star on the Hollywood Walk of Fame.

The shock and devastation was so huge that the other performers on that tour could still be moved to tears by the memories 50 years on. The whole thing seemed unbelievable. Such talent snuffed out way before it's time. Buddy's pregnant wife was so distressed that she miscarried their unborn child.

The tragedy was later immortalised as 'The Day the Music Died' by American singer/songwriter Don McLean in his famous song *American Pie.* Writing on his website, Don explains that his inspiration for the song came when he was thinking back over his life and remembered how he felt when, while earning pocket money as a paper boy, he cut open his bundle of newspapers for delivery and read the front page story of the deaths of Buddy Holly, Ritchie Valens and the Big Bopper. He recalls being in shock while he delivered the papers on his route, saying, 'Buddy's death, for me, an impressionable 13-year-old, was an enormous tragedy. The cover photo of the posthumously released *Buddy Holly Story* and the *Buddy Holly Story, Vol. 2*, coupled with liner notes written by his widow, María, created a sense of grief which lived inside of me, until I was able to exorcise it with the opening verse of *American Pie*. Through my relationship with Buddy, I was able to discover my peculiar writing talent and, much to my amazement, help bring Buddy and his music back from the dead. In a sense, *American Pie* contains the spiritual connection to Buddy Holly which was always in me. It's as if we both gave each other new life.'

American Pie came fifth in a poll of the 365 "Songs of the 20th Century" compiled by the Recording Industry Association of America and the National Endowment for the Arts.

Quite incredibly, Eddie Cochran, another brilliant young rock and roll star, would die while travelling only a year later, aged just 21. Eddie was towards the end of a British tour and returning from a performance at the Bristol Hippodrome when he was involved in a road accident in Wiltshire, dying afterwards at St Martin's Hospital in Bath.

His hit songs, including *Summertime Blues, C'Mon Everybody, Somethin' Else* and *Twenty Flight Rock*, featuring his experimentation with multi-track recording, sound distortion and overdubbing had probably assured him of a place in rock and roll history anyway, but his untimely death took him to iconic status. Often described as 'James Dean with a guitar', he inspired many artists from Marc Bolan and T. Rex to Pete Townshend and The Who.

A good-looking sharp dresser, with a rebellious attitude, he was a perfect pop star, with all-American-boy good looks. Although he only clocked up a couple of hits in native America, he was a big star in the UK where fans considered him, in the words of his own song, 'somethin' else'. He was inducted into the Rock and Roll Hall of Fame in 1987.

LEFT: Eddie Cochran

CHAPTER ELEVEN

The Legacy

1960 ONWARDS

Of course the music didn't literally die in 1959, but rock and roll did begin to fade away during the early years of the next decade.

'The times, they are a' changin'

In the 1960s, as Bob Dylan so aptly put it, 'The times, they are a' changin', and world events began to shift. Where rock and roll had a feel-good exuberance which matched the mood of an optimistic post-war West, the 1960s saw more social and political upheaval as the civil rights campaign geared up, Martin Luther King Jr and President John Kennedy were assassinated, and America became involved in the Vietnam War. Music began to reflect these changes, for example as folk-influenced protest and anti-war songs began to hit the charts.

Female and sexual liberation led to the decade becoming known as the Swinging Sixties. America felt low after the assassination of its glamourous young president Kennedy and was ripe for something fresh.

That fresh feel to music in America was delivered from Liverpool, UK, by four mop-headed young men, John, Paul, George and Ringo, together known as The Beatles.

With homegrown rock and roll having dominated America throughout the 1950s, British music hadn't troubled the charts too much. The success of Lonnie Donegan in 1955 had perhaps given a clue that the UK could 'sell coals to Newcastle' when his

repackaging of the old American Southern blues tune *Rock Island Line* made the charts. But since then Britain had merely conjured up some paler imitations of the American rock and roll pioneers and these UK stars never really made an impression on the American charts.

But The Beatles changed everything. The band was entirely original and insanely talented, but also zany and irreverent in wholesome and harmless ways. Their 1963 breakthrough, success and associated fan worship, christened Beatlemania, had inspired a news item in the States, following which fans began requesting their music on American radio. Several New York radio stations began playing *I Want to Hold Your Hand* on its release day and suddenly everything took off. The record sold one million copies in just ten days, and *Cashbox* magazine had certified the record #1 for the week ending 25 January, after just three weeks in their Top 100.

The death knell for the old rock and roll stars effectively rang out as The Beatles stepped off the plane in New York on 7 February 1964 on their first visit to America. They were greeted by astounding scenes as an estimated crowd of 5,000 fans screamed at them. 48 hours later an estimated 73 million viewers watched them sing on the Ed Sullivan show, although their songs were almost drowned out by more screaming, this time from the girls in the studio audience. Their set included their hit *I Want to Hold Your Hand, All My Loving* and *She Loves You,*

The appearance is considered a watershed moment in American pop. Their reign had begun. That's not to say the 1950s stars didn't continue to have hits in the early 60s – they did. But Buddy Holly was dead, Little Richard, Chuck Berry and Jerry Lee Lewis had each had their heydays and Elvis was stuck in the studio making movies which became increasingly middle of the road musically, and comedic, rather than dramatic in their content. The Everly Brothers crossed over from the late 50s to the 1960s with their rock and roll influenced country sound.

The Beatles were soon followed up the American charts by fellow Brits, The Rolling Stones, The Dave Clark Five, The Yardbirds, The Who, and Herman's Hermits. New American stars included Bob Dylan, James Brown, The Beach Boys, The Supremes, and The Byrds.

TOP RIGHT: The Stones at a Beverly Hills Press conference, 1965
MIDDLE RIGHT: The Dave Clark Five, 1964
BOTTOM RIGHT: The Yardbirds, 1965
ABOVE: The Who, 1965

But although it was definitely new, the British sound did display strong echoes of 1950s music. Rock and roll had been a formative influence on almost every successful British musician and certainly on all four members of The Beatles. So it was rather poignant and somewhat ironic that it was the incredible success of The Beatles and their contemporaries that came to redefine rock and roll and hasten the move towards more of a 'beat sound'.

Then, rock and roll began to sound even more moribund as The Beatles made incredible music advances by adding strings and new percussion, introducing concept albums and riffing off old jazz and folk tunes. And of course, new technology emerged to create new sounds that simply hadn't been possible in the 1950s, including stereo recording.

With the rock and rollers having established a strong demand for young music, that market understandably began to expand. New styles and trends took off, including Motown, folk, surf music, the Brill Building sound and Phil Spector's Wall of Sound.

The remaining Beatles and Rolling Stones, Elton John, Eric Clapton and the many other star musicians who had fallen under the spell of rock and roll in their youth are now elder statesman of the British and American music scene, so keeping the fire of rock and roll burning bright.

RIGHT: New York City policemen try to restrain hordes of teenagers from crashing into the Warwick Hotel, The Beatles' New York residence, August 12 1965.

abc

ABOVE: Carole King, Paul Simon (right) and Gerry Goffin (back) between takes in the Brill Building, New York, circa 1959

RIGHT: The Brill Building

THE BRILL BUILDING SOUND

Since the late 19th century, songwriters had been employed by the music publishing companies which lined West 28th street in New York, an area which came to be closely associated with the music industry as Tin Pan Alley.

But as the music industry developed, a new generation of songwriters sought their own stomping ground. Much of this was centred around offices in the 11-storey art deco Brill Building down in the heart of Broadway at 49th where the men and women who would shape 1950s and 60s R&R, R&B and pop music wrote, demoed and published their work.

Famous among the 'Brill Building' school of songwriters were influential talents still relevant today, including Carole King, Gerry Goffin, Neil Sedaka, Neil Diamond, Paul Simon and Phil Spector.

ABOVE: Robert Plant, John Paul Jones and Jimmy Page of Led Zeppelin at the Inglewood Forum in Los Angeles, California, 1977

Rock and roll, later evolving into rock music, is an art form, with enough depth and sophistication to warrant being a lifelong passion. So pervasive was its influence that it showed up in other cultural spheres including fashion, cinema, language, and helped to change social attitudes for the better. Indeed, because black and white Americans were united in their love of rock and roll, the music undoubtedly helped cement the move towards mainstream acceptance of black culture in America.

Of course, music has and will always continue to develop and take on new hues. But much of it still owes a massive debt to the irrepressible joyousness of 1950s, fresh and wild-eyed, rock and roll.

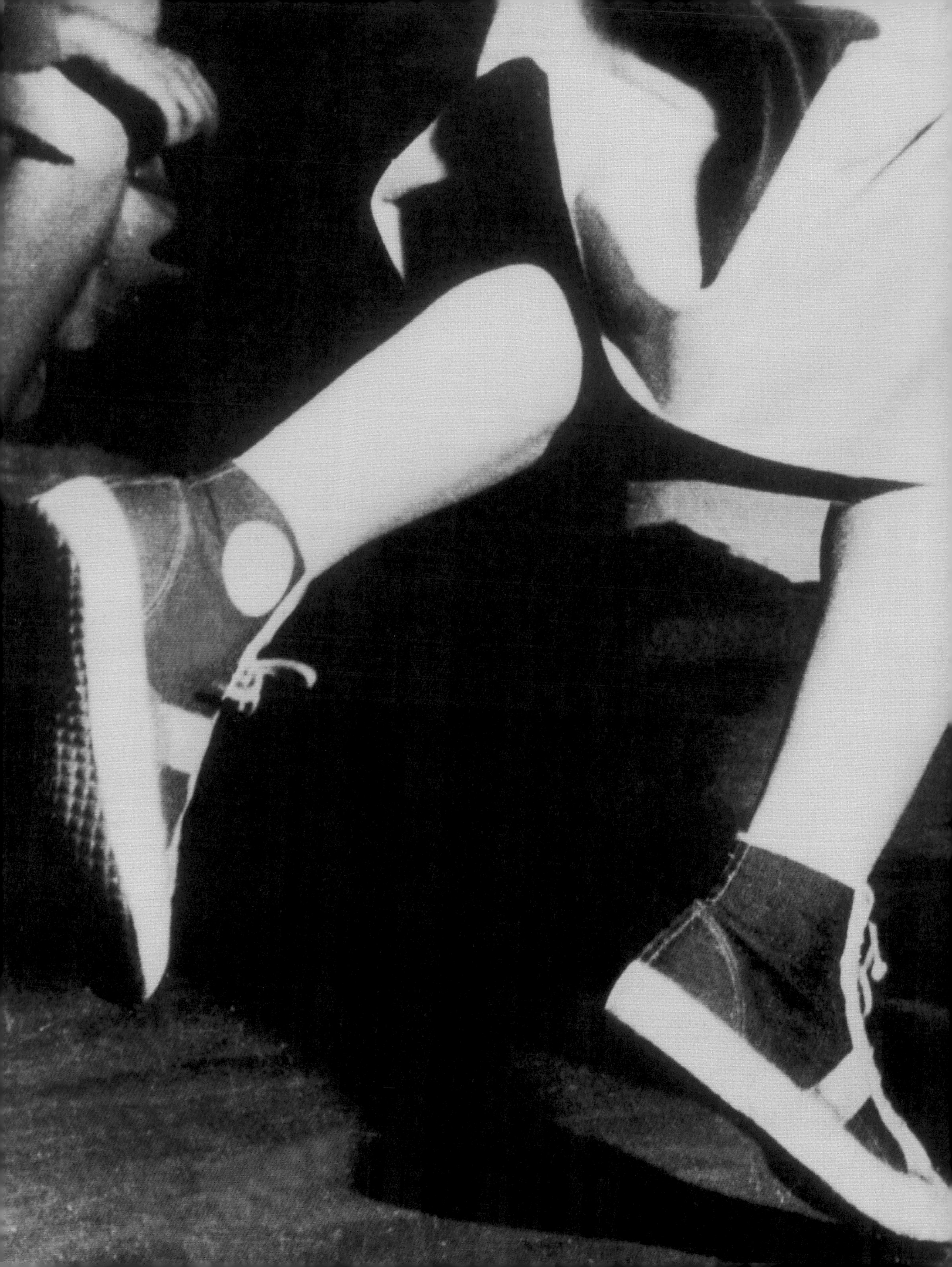